STORIES OF THE GODDESS
DIVINE FEMININE FREQUENCY KEEPERS

RADHAA NILIA

Copyright © 2023 by Radhaa Nilia, Radhaa Publishing House, Goddess Code Academy, Goddess Activations

All rights reserved.

No part of this book may be reproduced in any form or by any electronic or mechanical means, including information storage and retrieval systems, without written permission from the curator, except for the use of brief quotations in a book review.

INTRODUCTION

At its core, this book is about empowering women to tap into their unique power and wisdom. It is a celebration of the beauty and complexity of the divine feminine and a call to action for women everywhere to embrace their divine feminine frequency and use it to create positive change in the World.

For centuries, women have been marginalized, silenced, and dismissed. But as we awaken to the power of our divine feminine frequency, we reclaim our voices and power. We are stepping into our sovereignty and creating a world where women are celebrated and honored for their unique gifts and talents. As you read through the stories in this book, I hope you are inspired to explore your feminine frequency, embrace self-empowerment, and discover the unique ways it resonates within them.

Frequencies, the subtle yet potent vibrations that permeate every aspect of existence, hold within them the

INTRODUCTION

potential for transformation, healing, and growth. The divine feminine, a mystical and mesmerizing force that flows through every aspect of creation, holds the power of frequencies within it. And at the heart of this transformational power lies the role of the Frequency Keeper, the guardian, and custodian of the divine feminine and the frequencies that flow through her.

The importance of becoming a Frequency Keeper cannot be overstated in a world that often seems fraught with chaos and discord. The role of the Frequency Keeper is to raise and hold a higher frequency, to create a space of healing, peace, and harmony in a world that so desperately needs it. And while anyone can become a Frequency Keeper, women, in particular, are called to this path, for within them lies the portal of the divine.

To become a Frequency Keeper is to embark upon a path of self-discovery, healing, and growth that allows one to tap into the power of frequencies to connect with the subtle yet potent energies that flow through every aspect of existence and to use this power to promote positive change in the World.

At the heart of the Frequency Keeper's journey lies the understanding of the significance of frequencies and their connection to cosmic energy. All substance is made up of energy, and different frequencies correspond to different states of being. We can tap into the power of positive energy and healing by raising and holding a high frequency.

The journey of the Frequency Keeper requires courage, dedication, and a deep commitment to healing and growth. But the rewards are beyond measure for those called to this

INTRODUCTION

path. In becoming a Frequency Keeper, we become custodians of the frequencies held within ourselves.

In our exploration of the Goddesses and the Feminine throughout history, we witness the intricate phases of celebration, oppression, manipulation, and brutality that have marked their journey, ultimately leading us to the present HER-STORY. Now, more than ever, it is critical to uplift women's voices, share their stories, and reclaim their rightful place as the Divine Feminine.

Join us in unraveling the tales of these powerful beings and discovering the wisdom they hold for us today. As a Frequency Keeper means doing what you can to raise the frequency within you. It is important because the frequency of the planet affects the well-being of all living beings on it and because it can contribute to a better world. By focusing on raising your frequency, you improve your well-being and contribute to the well-being of others and the planet. Thank you for your positive intention to be a frequency keeper in our World.

Much Love,
Radhaa

CHAPTER I
THE RETURN OF THE GODDESS

By: RADHAA NILIA

"The history of the Goddesses and the Feminine is complex, marked by periods of adoration, suppression, and violence."

Once upon a time, there was a World where the feminine was worshiped and revered. The Goddesses were powerful, multifaceted, and essential to the survival and flourishing of societies. Women were seen as equal partners in creating and sustaining life. The earliest documented depictions of Goddesses can be traced back to the Upper Paleolithic era when small figurines of women with exaggerated breasts and hips were discovered. These Venus figurines are believed to have been associated with fertility, childbirth, nurturing, and in honor of the Mother.

But then, something happened. With the rise of Patriarchal societies, the role of the Goddesses began to change. As male Gods became more dominant, the Goddesses were often relegated to secondary or minor roles. In some cases, she was even demonized or marginalized in religious texts and myths.

For example, one of the most famous Goddesses in ancient history was Inanna, the Sumerian Goddess of love, fertility, war, and wisdom. Inanna was known not only for her beauty but also for her strength and power. She was revered by the people of Sumer as believed to have control over the cycle of life and death. Throughout Mesopotamian history, many myths and legends were about Inanna. One of the most important temples in the City of Uruk in southern Mesopotamia was built in remembrance of her-the largest and most important in the region. However, as the Patriarchal system took hold, Inanna's role diminished. She was eventually absorbed into the Babylonian pantheon, and her role was reduced to that of a 'fertility goddess' rather than the powerful and multifaceted Goddess she had once been. (Mesopotamia is an ancient eastern Mediterranean region often called the 'cradle of civilization.' It is located between the Tigris and Euphrates Rivers in what is now Iraq, and it is one of the earliest known civilizations in human history).

STORIES OF THE GODDESS

Goddess Suppression & Violence Against Women

THE SYSTEMATIC PERSECUTION of a million women accused of witchcraft is one of the most lethal DNA-altering examples that caused women severe trauma, a well-known historical fact of unacceptable heightened abuse caused by the Patriarch against the feminine.

Many women were healers, midwives, herbalists, caregivers, or other natural practitioners seen as threatening by the male-dominated medical establishment. By accusing these women of witchcraft, patriarchal authorities could suppress their knowledge and expertise, reinforcing male control over medicine.

The suppression of the Goddesses was not limited to Mesopotamia. In ancient Egypt, the Goddess Isis was one of the most popular deities, worshiped as a Mother and bringer of Life Goddess. However, as Egypt became more Patriarchal, male Gods such as Amun and Ra eventually overshadowed the Goddess Isis. In Greece, the Goddess Athena was one of the most revered deities, known for her wisdom, courage, and strength. Similarly, as Greek society became more patriarchal, Athena's role changed. She was often depicted as a 'virgin goddess,' symbolizing male control over female sexuality. (She was even portrayed as a male warrior--as if to emphasize that women were not fit to fight). As the suppression of the Goddess continued, women began to suffer under Patriarchal systems.

The suppression of the Goddess continued into the

Middle Ages when the Catholic Church actively worked to demonize pagan Goddesses and female deities. The witch hunts of the 16th and 17th centuries directly resulted from this, as the Church sought to eliminate any remnants of Goddess worship that still existed in Europe and various parts of the World, Goddess temples have been replaced by churches built over them, symbolizing ownership of the Divine Feminine and in a radical way of feeding the literal womb of the Goddess power energy. In some cases, the churches were built over the temples to assert the new religion's dominance over the ancient ways. It was often the case during the Christianization of the Roman Empire when pagan temples were converted into Christian churches.

You will never hear this information anywhere because it's a dirty secret that many churches of a different faith (Catholic or Islam) ruled by Patriarchy have been built over former Goddess temple sites in various parts of the World, including in Mesopotamia. This practice of building religious structures over the sites of earlier religious Goddess sites is known as "appropriation." Appropriation from Dictionary means: The act of appropriating or taking possession of something, often without permission or consent.

The Exploitation of Goddesses and The Feminine

One of the most demeaning aspects of the suppression of the Goddess is how it was often carried out through religious texts and mythology.

The most egregious examples of the suppression of the Goddess can be found in the Bible. In many cases, the Goddess was demonized or marginalized in myths and stories, or her role was reduced to that of a secondary or minor character. For example, in the story of Adam and Eve, the female character is depicted as the one who brings about the downfall of humanity, who took the knowledge of sin and infected the World. In contrast, the male character is portrayed as the innocent victim. This demonization and marginalization of women and Goddesses are not unique to Western culture.

While there are many stories of strong and powerful women in the Bible, their stories are often overshadowed by the Patriarchal narrative that dominates the text. For example, the story of Lilith, who was said to be Adam's first wife, has been largely erased from the Bible. According to legend, Lilith refused to submit to Adam's will and was cast out of the Garden of Eden. Her powerful story has inspired many women to stand for their sovereign rights.

Another example of the suppression of the Goddess can be found in the story of Mary Magdalene. While Mary Magdalene is one of the most important figures in Christian mythology, the Church largely overlooked or marginalized her role. Mary Magdalene has even been portrayed as a prostitute rather than the powerful and influential figure she truly was. However, in recent years, there has been a renewed interest in Mary Magdalene, and many women have been inspired by her story to reclaim their power and authority.

In Chinese mythology, many stories depict women and

the Goddess in a negative light or as subordinate to male Gods and figures. Similarly, in the story of Pandora's Box, the female character is blamed for all the World's evils, while the male characters are absolved of any responsibility. The exploitation of Women became a grandiose built-in reality in the 3D matrix.

The Resurgence of Interest in The Goddess

THE RESURGENCE of interest in the Goddess as women seek to reclaim their power and place in society is rising. Knowing that the suppression of the Goddess on Earth directly resulted from Patriarchal systems that sought to eliminate female power and control is a tragedy. Yet, despite the efforts to suppress the Goddess, Her influence continued to be felt.

The feminist movement of the 1960s and 1970s played a significant role in the resurgence of interest in Goddesses. This movement helped spark a renewed interest in Goddess worship, and neo-paganism has provided a framework for incorporating Goddess worship into modern spiritual practices. Feminist scholars and writers such as Gloria Steinem and Carol P. Christ highlighted the importance of Goddess worship and the need to reclaim the feminine divine. It led to the formation of feminist spirituality groups, which sought to explore and celebrate the role of the Goddess in women's lives.

One of the most significant contributions of the feminist spirituality movement was the creation of new rituals and practices that honored the Devine feminine. These rituals were often based on ancient Goddess traditions but adapted to modern contexts. They included practices such as women's circles, where women would gather to share their experiences and support each other, and Goddess ceremonies, which celebrated the cycles of the moon and the seasons connected to their creation of life and blood.

The resurgence of interest in the Goddess also impacted

feminist theology. Feminist theologians began to explore the role of the feminine divine in traditional religions, challenging the male-centric interpretations of scripture and doctrine. They argued that the suppression of the Goddess was not just a historical phenomenon but also a continuing reality in modern religions. They called for a reimagining of theology that centered on the Divine feminine and valued women's experiences and perspectives.

Re-emergence of the Goddess

The re-emergence of the Goddess has also had an impact on popular culture. The image of the strong, powerful woman has become a popular trope in books, movies, and television shows. Characters such as Wonder Woman, Xena, and Buffy the Vampire Slayer embody the archetype of the warrior Goddess fighting against injustice, oppression, and the dark matrix.

The Goddess's influence has persisted throughout history and continues to influence us today through the women's movement in the West. We can also see this continuum of Goddess worship through India's ancient culture of the East and other Asian countries being cultivated to this current timeline through rituals, honor, and respect given to their Goddesses from ancient times.

The progress made in reclaiming the Goddess is not over yet. There are still challenges. The Patriarchal systems that suppressed the Goddess still exist, and women still face discrimination and inequality in many areas of life. We must recognize that the suppression of the Goddesses has profoundly affected women throughout history. Women have often been denied education, healthcare, and other basic rights due to Patriarchal systems that seek to maintain control over them.

However, the interest in the Goddess Worldwide ignites unstoppable inspiration and empowerment for women, reminding them of their place as "Equal partners in creating and sustaining life in society."

This re-emergence of interest in the Goddess has taken many forms, from neo-pagan ism to feminist spirituality to celebrating ancient Goddess traditions. Women are reclaiming their stories, histories, and power, and the Goddess is once again taking her rightful place at the center of our spiritual and cultural lives. In remembering, the suppression of the Goddess may have been a tragic and complex story that has profoundly affected women's self-confidence throughout history. Despite centuries of suppression, the Goddess has persisted, and her influence can be felt today. By exploring the history of the Goddess, we can gain a deeper understanding of how Patriarchy seeks to maintain control over women. We can also greatly appreciate women and Goddesses' enduring strength and resilience. As we continue to explore the stories and traditions of the Goddess, we can also gain insight into our own lives and how we can reclaim our power and autonomy.

Ancient to Future Goddess Stories

It is important to recognize that the Goddess's story is not just a story of the past. Women continue to face inequality and oppression in many parts of the World, and the fight for gender equality is far from over. However, by reclaiming the stories and traditions of the Goddesses, women can gain a sense of empowerment and connection to something larger than themselves. The Goddess represents the power and strength of women, and the Goddess story is a reminder that women have always been a force to be reckoned with. From the fierce warrior Goddesses of ancient mythology to modern-day women fighting for justice and equality, the Goddess continues to inspire and empower women worldwide. Ultimately, the Goddess's story is a story of hope and resilience.

Our Goddess Story, Work of the Goddess

The story of the Goddess is our story. Embracing the Feminine Soul's voice guides women toward their Dharma and Purpose to speak their deep-down wisdom and truth. It deserves to be told and celebrated for generations to come. Despite centuries of suppression and oppression, the Goddess has endured, and her influence can be felt throughout our lives today. As we continue to write the Goddess's story, we must remain mindful and vigilant of how Patriarchy seeks to suppress and silence women. We must also remain committed to fighting for gender equality and work toward a future where women and Goddesses are celebrated and honored in all their power and glory.

As Maya The Shaman shares in her icon of Remembering
"It's our time to remember!"

By embracing the stories and traditions of the Goddess, women can reclaim their power and autonomy and work towards a future in which gender equality is a reality for all. The resurgence of interest in the Goddess by women seeking to reclaim their power, sovereignty, and place in society in the 20th century helped spark a continued growing movement. Despite having a complex history of the Goddess marked by periods of adoration and suppression, women will always remember.

The Divine Feminine Frequency Keepers: Remembering Our Birthright

---

As women, we are conditioned to internalize the patriarchal lies of not being good enough, too raw, or too real. We are taught to be perfect and palatable, to remain in the polite good girl skin. But as Audre Lorde said, **"Your silence will not protect you."** My work revolves around dismantling these limiting beliefs and embracing our soul voice, which guides us toward our Dharma and speaks our deep-down wisdom.

As we journey through life, we encounter moments of reflection and introspection that lead us to uncover hidden truths about ourselves. For many women, this journey requires tapping into their divine feminine frequency and exploring the unique ways it resonates within them.

The divine feminine frequency represents the powerful and transformative energy that exists within every woman. It is the essence of our being that is inextricably linked to the cycles of nature, the ebbs and flows of the Universe, and the ever-present force of creation. As women, it is our birthright to tap into this frequency and harness its power to create positive change in our lives and the World. However, the journey toward fully embracing and embodying our divine feminine frequency can be challenging and fraught with obstacles and self-doubt.

That is why I decided to curate the book, "Stories of the Goddess: Divine Feminine Frequency Keepers," a collection of stories from women around the World who have tapped into their divine feminine frequency and are using it to create positive change in their lives and the lives of others.

Maya Angelou once said, **"There is no greater agony than bearing an untold story inside you."** We use writing and storytelling to heal the feminine wounds and practice being seen and heard.

Summary

As you know, the Goddess is non-linear, and so are her stories. These stories remind us of the many ways the Goddess shows up in our lives, guiding us, nurturing us, and empowering us to be our truest selves. Each woman's story is a unique expression of the divine feminine, and together they create a vibrant tapestry of spiritual wisdom and inspiration. We see the Goddess in the natural world: birth, growth, death, and Rebirth Cycles. We feel her presence in the depths of our souls, urging us to listen to our intuition and follow our hearts. As we honor the Goddess in all her forms, we honor the sacredness of all life and the interconnectedness of all beings. We recognize that we are all part of a larger cosmic dance, and each has a unique role in the universe's unfolding. May these stories inspire you to connect with the Goddess within yourself and embrace the beauty and power of the divine feminine in all its manifestations.

    Much Love,
    Radhaa

RADHAA NILIA

ABOUT THE AUTHOR

Radhaa Nilia is a Publishing Priestess who supports writers in bringing their stories to life and becoming successful authors. As the founder of Radhaa Publishing House, she creates sacred writing containers to help authors birth their books and activate their inner genius. Radhaa has launched multiple best-selling books and provides ongoing support to authors in visibility, publicity, and book signings. She is a seeker, advocates for diverse voices, and a lifelong teacher of the Goddess Archetypes. Radhaa's passion for empowering women extends beyond writing and publishing. She founded the Goddess Code Academy as a transformative platform that offers courses and programs focused on exploring the Divine Feminine. Recently, Radhaa merged the Academy and Publishing under the umbrella of the Goddess Code Collective, bringing forward the modern Neo-Renaissance. This collective provides a safe and supportive space where women come together to share their experiences, learn from one another, and support each other's personal and professional growth on the monthly calls. Radhaa cherishes learning and sharing; her mission is to help people remember who they truly are. She believes every person has a unique story to tell, and she is dedicated to helping them find their voice and bring their stories to the world. With events, workshops, and online resources, the Goddess Code Collective is a powerful community of women who uplift and empower one another.

www.RadhaaPublishingHouse.com
www.GoddessCodeCollective.com
www.RadhaaNilia.Net

CHAPTER 2
CHANNELING HATHOR

By: JOAN of ANGELS

Channeling Hathor (Merging With The Divine)

As I invoke the prayer clearing all negative energies, this life, past life, and future lives, I am simultaneously living in Egypt, in the sleeping body of the giant Goddess Hathor, melding into this period with Joan of Angels. Powerful memories of leaving Atlantis to establish mystery schools across the globe and birth the great civilization of Egypt return, confirming early childhood memories of past lives during my session with Radhaa on her Goddess Activations.

I saw myself as the Goddess of Love and Beauty, the

Cosmic Channel between Heaven and Earth. I am the Mother of the pharaohs and the grandmother of the ancients. As the consort to Ra, the Sun God, and Horus, the Sky God, I walk among the sky deities as their Oracle and Muse. When the days of the ancient Gods were complete, Egypt and much of the ancient World descended into darkness. It was predicted that with the beginning of the Aquarian age, enlightenment would commence, and we, from the future, would awaken the sleeping ones we once were.

Years ago, in a vision clear as night, I found myself swimming toward the Oracle of Delphi. The great God Poseidon was on my right, as was my beloved dog, Bear, both statues underwater, hundreds of feet high. Instead of arriving on land, mermaids escorted me and guided me deep below into a vast underwater Olympian temple. The banquet tables were filled to the brim with food fit for the Gods and delicacies to bring delight. Each deity my eyes beheld was dressed in golden iridescent threads adorned with jewels and embedded with high-frequency energy. In the presence of the Gods of old, I was welcomed to my rightful place at this divine table as a beloved family member returning home.

What a night, dancing with the Gods, swept up in a whirlwind of celestial twists and twirls till we spun off the planet. I thought the ancient Gods had left this planet long ago, but little did I know they were suspended underwater. They have been waiting for you and me to awaken, as the energies of the Goddess are needed now to stabilize humanity in these times of transition.

The thousand-year state of suspension has come to an end. Watch now as the Goddess returns to her glory and takes charge of rebirthing the upgraded spiritual human, replacing the outdated DNA with new templates and codes containing powerful angelic origins.

With the turning of time, both the giants and Gods went deep inside Gaia, either in suspended animation or were fossilized, waiting till humanity awakens to their divine history, and it is safe to remember. Those who place their ears on the Earth say the Mother is shaking as the giants are stirring.

Ancient prophecies tell us the Gods will awaken soon when the breath of life flows over them. You are in the process of remembering the Goddess you embody and with whom you share soul resonance. Your life breath awakens the Goddess of old, animating its body and activated solely by you. These are the times you have been called and for whom the Goddess is calling. That which you are here to do now in this timeline, you have done in past lives as a priestess, a Goddess, an oracle, or a scribe. The higher dimensional skills you mastered then are now easily accessible. These memories are a gift from the divine and a sacred treasure. Many are called, but few choose.

As I claim my Goddess of the Heavens and the Celestial Realms, I invoke wisdom and hope to flow from above, inspiring you to step into your full power. You will feel the presence of the angels unlocking your yoke and chains. Feel the return of your memories of walking these lands in a time long ago as you breathe life into your form. The Goddess brings gratitude, compassion, and beauty, encouraging you to continue despite your heavy burdens. The values of harmony, peace, and balance have been spread across the land, enabling all beings to live in alignment with the cosmic source of creation.

As Joan, I have always known my mission is to heal, inspire, and uplift humanity by radiating my true light and angelic presence. I have been trained to trust and become this radiant light of love, never dimming my flame as humanity upgrades its activated individual angelic templates.

In my vision, I merged with Hathor while meditating at my desk. By extending my roots down to the Earth's center, I feel Hathor's feet open and become one with my feet. My antenna extends from my crown through the Goddess's crown, going directly to the heavens. I am inside a rather large marble statue hundreds of feet high. The humans far below are like ants scrambling about. I cannot tell one from another.

My Soul's mission is to do what I have always done, turn on your gifts, superpowers, and memories to do your work now.

"I am one with the Goddess," and the Goddess Activations I had with Radhaa is complete. I have walked the planet as the high priestess of Atlantis, as Huan Yin, Mother of Kwan Yin/Quan Yin, and as the daughter of Cleopatra. My assignment throughout each life was to raise the vibratory frequency of humanity, one person at a time, before I left the planet. This has been confirmed in several visions and plant medicine ceremonies and during a regression studying why I was called to Baja. During this session, I was shown my mission of turning up every person's power and light, just like I used to do at the end of each chiropractic adjustment when I'd say, "Power On!"

Hathor is a creator Goddess and has been here since the beginning. She holds divine energy, as do all the deities. During contact, our DNA is altered, and our vibration lifts. We become a higher dimensional being aligned with the Gods. As we awaken, the Gods wake up.

Egyptians revered those virtues of peace, balance, and harmony for empowering society, which all Egyptians aspire to. The Goddess held these energies steady for all people. I speak as one designated to bring cosmic light to the planet during struggle and difficulty. During times of darkness and great hardships such as now, the Goddess plays a critical role in distracting the public from their misery by infusing them with hope and beauty. As a young girl, my guides told me it was necessary to build my confidence to radiate a sense of knowingness and leadership, whether I was aware of it or not.

I remember a recurring childhood dream in which I carried a beautiful white marble statue wherever I was. For many years, I thought maybe that statue was my Mother, but now I suspect she was Hathor. Recently my Mother told me I am the daughter of Cleopatra and come from a long lineage of beautiful women with shapely legs. My father married my Mother because of her extraordinary good looks. My grandmother Fanny used to model hats for my grandfather, a milliner. My Mother modeled Grandpa's high couture designer fashions and ran his showroom in the garment center of New York City. As a child, I secretly longed to be a model and actress despite being extremely shy and hid in my closet for fear of being seen.

My lineage emulates beauty in a dark world. I've experienced this skill when dressed in my colors and looking divinely attractive. I silently enter the room so as not to be noticed. That rarely happens as something in my energy field, along with how I walk, alerts people to my light-filled presence. The Goddess energy allows others to feel nurtured, safe and protected when you are in their divine presence. You cannot take the Goddess out of yourself. This power is within you 24/7 as a core nugget. The Egyptians were allowed to step into this divine state of grace by praying to the Gods.

Growing up, it was clear that being beautiful wasn't all it was cracked up to be. My father was extremely verbally abusive and turned his wrath on Mom. All sparks of enthusiasm were drained from her. She was to be seen and not heard. I did not want to follow in her footsteps. Other memories of losing my life from other lives for being a healer, a witch, an oracle, or one who spoke to the gods, kept me from knowing who I am. In one lifetime, the king was outraged when I spoke to the Gods, as only he had that privilege. In anger, he ordered four strong guards to drag me to the top of the pyramid and hold me down on the altar, ready to sacrifice my heart to his gods. Spittle dripped from the king's mouth as he raised his dagger above my body. At the last moment, I wrenched free from the grasp of the four guards and leaped over the side of the pyramid to my death, depriving the king of his sacrifice.

Healers threatened the priestly class, especially since women's herbal treatments were more effective than the brutal religious blood forced upon brainwashed patients. Wise women were burned at the stake, as were the oracles, the healers, doctors, and truth-sayers. Many lifetimes of persecution I experienced because of my rebellious nature when I couldn't see, hear, sense, touch, or speak. Those who knew how to harmonize with the Earth were targeted for destruction. No wonder these memories must be ripped away like a bandage, stripping away loose skin if needed. It is now safe to reawaken these memories. You, the Goddess, are awakening to the gifts and skills you came here to use. Your Soul's purpose is to be your true self now and shine your light.

In my early twenties, following a call from my guides, I moved cross country to a Spiritual Community in Los Angeles. After moving into the Ashram, I became an initiate and minister in the Movement of Spiritual Inner Awareness. Except for me, each minister was given a special healing gift for their ministry. My special gift was that people would be healed by being present in a room. Now I understand, but back then, it was an enigma. There was nothing for me to do or be. I merely needed to show up and be me.

At 30, I received a life-changing vision. I was on stage in front of the Colosseum while millions of people were crawling by or walking with crutches or wheelchairs. I was clothed as my celestial self, and behind me was a tall angelic being. As we waved our arms and wands over the masses, each human stood up, framed in the light, and instantly healed. They dropped their crutches and moved forward into their destiny, fully recovered. At that moment, I knew I was here to heal and inspire large groups of humanity and reach many people. What does that mean? As Hathor's embodiment connecting Heaven and Earth, we are here to assist you in raising the frequency of Love, Beauty, and Joy. We represent the cosmetic arts so women can tastefully beautify their senses and smell and experience love, play, sacred sexuality, dance, and music. We are here to express and emulate these arts so humanity can become like the Goddess. This is our gift to assist you in experiencing your divinity. You begin by seeing yourself connected to us and allowing the merging to occur. See yourself in the body of Hathor or Ra, whichever deity calls, and align the cords of your feet with the center of the Earth and your antenna to the heavens. When the alignment has occurred, you will feel the divine power is turned on and flowing through you.

Hathor held the gifts of compassion, kindness, and forgiveness. She knew humanity needed to see and be reminded of the blessings and beauty in their daily lives to overcome their trials and tribulations amid the darkest and deepest of despair. Each follower of Hathor was taught the Five Gifts of Gratitude. They were taken before the priest and told to take out their arm and look at each finger. The priest asked who you would think of and miss the most should you die and leave your body right now? Who or what would bring heartbreak when you left? Is it your children, spouse, friends, or home?

I would miss those I've helped and those I haven't yet reached. I am grateful to be here and have been able to do the work. I would miss my family, my friends, and all of you. Each morning upon awakening, give gratitude to your family, children, and loved ones and thank those who have worked with you in this life, past and future lives as you continue to raise your vibration frequency. I am grateful to all the angels on the planet who choose to connect to their celestial and divine selves. We thank you for your presence here with us and remind you of your gifts of gratitude. Using my skills as priestess and the energy of Goddess Hathor and as Joan, I could chant the sacred Egyptian tones to merge with Hathor. The ancient magicians used these chants to invoke and awaken the presence of the gods by literally stepping inside the marble body of Hathor. By sending my roots down through the center of Hathor's feet into the center of the Earth and my antenna through the crown and into the heavens, I become activated as Hathor.

I experienced a whirring sound as the body of Hathor was suddenly activated, turned on, and awakened from that suspended state of animation. My presence as Joan was the conduit to connect heaven and Earth, and the divine energies of love, balance, and harmony flowed through me as the past, present and future timelines merged into the now. We ask you to feel the presence of your heart right now, this connection to the divine ones, awakening both as an ancient one and yet in your body today. Your freedom is only a breath away. As your memories return, there is an alignment through past life, present, and future timelines. It is now when we, and the Gods, are waking up and being embodied by you, the Goddess. You are being called to awaken to your highest and best self. Will you say Yes?

And so it is.

JOAN OF ANGELS

ABOUT THE AUTHOR

Joan of Angels is the Oracle of Ancient Wisdom, with a soul mission to help you REMEMBER who you truly are, unlock your highest potential and support you as you step into your sovereignty. She acts as a Spiritual Advisor to help you rewire your subconscious mind, release fear, and step into your true mastery and highest potential. Also known as Dr. Joan Hangarter, and was trained as a Doctor of Chiropractic and earned an MS in Counseling. She was gifted with the name

Joan of Angels because she is very connected with the angelic and galactic realms, helps people find their way, and is now a Spiritual Chiropractor who helps adjust things that are no longer in alignment that keep us from tapping into our inner wisdom. She has been channeling these Earth Messengers ever since she was instructed to paint 33 angels in 30 days and is renowned for her visionary art and Soul essence portraits. As a Public Speaker, Joan speaks on personal transformation, stepping into one's power and potential, working with the energy body, the Soul's journey, and Star Seed /Life Purpose Mission Activations. She loves connecting her clients to their guides so they can directly receive this guidance.

Check out her weekly show, Miracle Monday, live on YouTube at **www.youtube.com/c/JoanofAngels** or visit her website at **www.joanofangels.com** and receive your free ebook on living your Soul filled purpose.

CHAPTER 3
THE GIFTS OF FREYJA

By: **MICHELLE NOBLE, LMT, BF, CFMW**

The Unexpected Energies of Motherhood

T he first time I gave birth, I was 37 years old. From a medical perspective, they call that "Advanced Maternal Age" or "Geriatric Pregnancy," meaning there is a higher risk for various complications.

What it meant for me was I'd had plenty of time to collect fixed points of view and conclusions, fantasies based on movies and books, and expectations based on other people's pregnancies, births, and experiences of motherhood. I was a massage therapist, steeped in alternative medicine, and committed to doing everything "naturally." Planning a home birth, I'd read all the books about how hospitals were scary places, full of interventions while holding a secret agenda to trick women into C-sections.

Holding firm to my belief that giving birth was something my Body should know how to do, I only wanted to focus on the positive. Positive thinking - that's how I would avoid the bad and get everything to work out as I wanted.

Did you notice that nowhere in any of that did I ask any questions?

Questions like, "Hey Body, where would you like to give birth? Hey Baby, where and how and when would you like to be born? What would make this experience the most ease and joy for all of us? How can I and my Body and my Baby work as a team to create something magical here? How can we (me, my Body, my Baby) receive the gifts others would like to give and be (like my husband or the midwives)?"

You see, it never occurred to me to get truly curious and be in a state of wonder. I needed to feel I had all the answers already. I needed to feel like I was driving the train. I didn't want to look at anything that would show me how little I was in control. So as my due date ticked by, I kept a smile on my face and read up on how normal it is for first pregnancies to go long. We inflated the birth tub in the living room as a test run. My husband and I sat in it and grinned at each other. We got this! We're prepared!

At around 41 ½ weeks, at 1:00 am or so in the morning, I woke to a gush of water soaking my Body. Jostling my husband awake, I said, "My water just broke! Get me a towel!" He leaped into action, disappearing for an extraordinarily long time and returning with a washcloth and a small hand towel, unsure which tiny item would be best for this job!

Eventually, we got me situated with a giant Kotex. I called my mom across the state, dumping about a thousand excited words on her sleep-sluggish brain, until a plan emerged that she would wake my step-dad and meet up with my sister, and they would all head our way in a couple of hours.

In the movies, this would be the part where contractions kick in quickly, the Mama groans, sweats (a little), and bears down, the adoring husband dabs the laboring woman's brow, the midwife does their part, and the camera cuts to the new family cradling their beautiful Baby...all in about 7-10 minutes of screen time. That's not what happened.

Instead, hours went by with no contractions, just plenty of waiting and maxi-pad changes. We took a walk. We cuddled. When we noticed the fluid was a funny color, we called the midwife, and she told us to come to her office. With compassionate professionalism, she told us that the funny color was meconium, which meant the Baby had pooped in utero, which could cause respiratory problems at birth if the Baby breathed in meconium particles. She recommended we go to the hospital. I was devastated and scared. What happened to my natural home birth plan? It felt like a huge loss and a risk to go to the hospital.

After this, the timeline gets blurry. I remember checking in to the hospital. Lots of walking and only light contractions. A Pitocin drip creates more crampy contractions. The hospital midwife saying I was not in active labor. Me resisting the urge to throat-punch her. Lots of hours. Exhaustion. My husband, by my side, is doing his best but is also exhausted. My family is arriving and finding a place to stay. The stupidly small hospital birth tub. Asking myself, "If I get an epidural, will I regret it?" and getting the answer, "No, you will think you were a very smart woman."

A million more hours while my husband got a hold of the midwife so she could order the epidural. The epidural helping, but now I'm stuck in bed, and labor is still not progressing quickly. C-section paperwork, "Just in case." Finally, something is happening. My Baby is in the birth canal. I'm trying to figure out how to push. My sister told me it's like pooping. An incredibly kind OB with slender hands. Vacuum. Forceps. "Quiet everyone, we want to make sure her airways are clear before she cries." Quiet. Clear. They are checking her. My husband is with her and, "When can I have her? Can I have her yet?" And I can, and she is here, and she is Rosemary.

When Rosemary was born, although I was 37 and a healer for many years, I was just beginning to learn about being me. If you had asked me to describe my most valuable qualities, I would have said, "I'm a good listener. I care about people. I'm responsible and helpful. I'm nice to others and am a good friend."

I remember hearing my sister-in-law say, "Until I had kids, I never knew I could feel such rage!" I was like, "What? I don't think that will be true for me. I'm so patient and even-tempered."

There's another saying, "People plan. God laughs." Rosemary kicked my ass. I am so grateful.

STORIES OF THE GODDESS

Getting to Know Freyja

WHEN I WAS INVITED to participate in *Stories of the Goddess*, I thought I'd write about what we can learn about motherhood from Mother Earth. I was interested in exploring that theme, but I could perceive the presence of another Goddess who was clear in her desire to be part of my chapter.

I hung out with her for a while, expanded my awareness, relaxed, and let go of what I thought this would be. I asked, "Who are you?"

"Freyja." Okay...

I'd heard of Freyja, but I needed clarity about who she was, so, like the modern wise woman I am, I Googled. Wikipedia answered: "Freyja (Old Norse "(the Lady) is a Goddess associated with love, beauty, fertility, sex, war, gold, and seidr (magic for seeing and influencing the future)."

I began to laugh. All of the energies of motherhood, even the spicy ones. Even the shadow ones. Even the ones who never make it into the "good mom" meme-o-sphere on social media. The ones we embrace when we, as women and Mothers, are willing to show up with whatever is required, not just the acceptable bits.

This is why I am so grateful for Rosemary, my fierce, intense, sensitive, highly aware Baby that is now growing into an extraordinary young woman.

Before Rosemary, I had built my life around being nice and easy to be around. Occasionally I'd made a choice that caused upset for others, but then I quickly went to work using all my soothing gifts to bring back calm and equilibrium.

Anger - bad. Rage - never. Fierceness - in moderation and politely. Love, Beauty, Fertility, Sex, Desire, Orgasmic Living - of course, in books and movies, but I have to work and cook dinner. War????? - that's unreasonable. Gold - just enough for a nice holiday now and again and never enough to make others uncomfortable (don't be too successful, others might feel bad).

And Seidr - I've always had so much magic for seeing and influencing the future, but acknowledging it seemed crazy. Arrogant. Besides, if I acknowledged my magic, I might also have to acknowledge my potency and quit pretending I was pathetic and trying so hard while still staying bound within normalcy.

But then I became a Mother, the hardest and most intense thing I'd ever experienced. Slowly, I began to learn: be Freyja or die. My daughter insisted that I show up fully and be present. Motherhood required me to shed my nice-nice skin. And I had it all - anger, rage, fury, hopelessness, helplessness, and I was so tired. But she wouldn't let me off the hook. She wouldn't let me stay small. Hers was the demand, "Mom, I chose you for a reason. BE YOU. Step up your game!"

So I have, not just for her sake, but also for my own.

And all those identities I believed were of value to me: the helper, the responsible one, the reasonable one, the nice one you could count on? I now know those are energies and capacities I can use, but they are not me, and they are not my value.

Learning Motherhood Choices

By the time Rosemary was preschool age, I was starting to make different choices. We had childcare so I could have time for myself and my business. I was learning motherhood included intensity and patience, that boundaries are acceptable, as are tears (mine and others), and to be kinder to myself when I made a mess of things. I also learned that sometimes messes are required, and perfectionism is self-annihilation and not particularly kind to anyone - me, my husband, or my child.

After the difficult birth, the postpartum depression and struggle, and the fact we were finally gaining some equilibrium, it seemed crazy to have another child. But the beauty, mystery, and possibility of adding another being to our lives wouldn't leave me alone. I couldn't let go of that curiosity and wonder, so after a miscarriage, I got pregnant again.

One of my choices was going to a holistic business development retreat in Florida when I was about two months pregnant. It wasn't an easy choice because I was having some bleeding, and with a history of miscarriages in two previous pregnancies, it brought up some fear. However, my fetal medicine doctor said the retreat would give me space to relax without the stress of family life. He said traveling would not put the pregnancy at greater risk, so I went.

During the retreat, one of the women shared a story that would give me a new awareness about my birth experience with Rosemary. When she went into the hospital with her first child's birth, she felt she had a good relationship with her doctor, and my friend felt supported. But her doctor's behavior changed as her birth went along, perhaps taking longer than expected. When my friend contacted the doctor from her room phone to ask questions about what was happening, she was shocked by how the doctor responded. She was treated as if she was out of line and unreasonably "questioning the doctor's recommendations."

At first, my friend was bewildered and devastated. She couldn't believe what had just happened!

Then she remembered she had tools she could use. She shifted her point of view and asked herself to acknowledge that everyone in the hospital was doing the best they knew how to do at that moment for the wellbeing of her and her Baby. She cleared her energy, connected with her truth, and relaxed her barriers.

Shortly after that, the doctor returned. It was like a switch had been flipped. The doctor was kind and apologetic, willing to listen and answer my friend's questions. She proceeded to give birth and welcome her Baby into the world, and she knew that it was HER OWN choice to drop her barriers, open and receive support, that allowed the doctor to change into someone who could offer it.

Hearing her story, I recognized that I had not been open during my hospital time for Rosemary's birth. Even when the nurses, the hospital midwife, and the doctors intended to support me, I could not receive that support. I was guarded, looking for traps.

Wow. Where else in my life was I doing that?

By the time I got home from Florida, the bleeding had stopped. A follow-up ultrasound showed my Baby was healthy. The rest of my pregnancy proceeded well, but I still had fear from the previous difficult birth. Now, though, I was willing to claim and receive what I required. When the impending birth stressed our relationship, my husband and I got counseling and became more vulnerable. We hired a hypnotherapist and doula so I would have tools to handle my fears and a caregiver I trusted with me at every stage, whether we had our planned home birth or ended up in the hospital.

On the day my second daughter was due, for fun and distraction, I went to an intro class for something called Access Consciousness®. I'd heard from two women I respected that Access had made more of a difference for them than anything else they'd tried. Faced with becoming the mom of a newborn and a "spirited" four-year-old while still desiring to grow my healing business, deepen my relationship with my husband, nurture my Body, and have more of me... let's say I was looking for powerful magic.

Throughout the class that evening, I immediately saw the simplicity and effectiveness of the Access® tools: tools to trust myself, to choose more easily, and to know that my inner-knowing was good and that I truly did know. I went home that night, and my water broke.

This time my labor progressed more quickly. When the doula arrived early the next morning and saw how I was doing, she called the midwives and told them they best come to our house sooner than later. I rocked, I walked, and I moaned deep in my Body. My husband was there with me. We were in our home. Rosemary's "Second Mom," Holli, arrived to keep her company, sit in her room, or take her to visit our neighbor if she got overwhelmed. Things got more intense. And then there started to be meconium in the amniotic fluid.

The midwife let us know what was happening, spoke about the risks, and asked us what we wanted to do. It was different than the first time; labor was progressing. There may have been less meconium showing up. Should we stay or go to the hospital? Our choice. My husband turned to me. He trusted me. Ultimately my choice.

But now I knew that my inner-knowing was good. I now had different tools. I checked in with my Body. I checked in with my Baby. Going to the hospital was not required. I told them we would stay. It would be alright. And it was.

After that, there was still a lot to be done. In and out of the birth tub, different positions, a little oxygen boost for the Baby and me (as we both were working hard), and encouragement from my husband, the doula, and the midwives. Baby's coming. Here's her head. Rosemary watched from a bit away. She's coming. Right away, she's here on my Body, and we're all together. Welcome, Gussy. Sweet Baby. Sweet, sweet Baby. You did it. We did it. Here is your Daddy. Here is your Sister. You're here!

Mother Earth to Gifts of Motherhood

As I mentioned, I wanted to write this chapter about what we can learn about motherhood from Mother Earth. And that is still part of this chapter. Like Freyja, the Earth does not have a point of view that fierceness, potency, death, sex, abundance, or pleasure are inappropriate or judgeable energies in creation. Earth will be the gentleness that allows a seed to sprout, a fruit to ripen, a lioness to lick the birth sack away from her cub's nose, and let a Baby come to her Mother's breast.

The Earth will also be the fire that rages across a forest so it can be reborn, that same lioness growling at her cub to leave off nipping at her Body, the fruit dropping to the ground to rot, and a Baby crying at the discomfort of a world colder and louder than the womb. In all this, the Earth will not feel guilty, doubtful, or ashamed; She will be whatever energy is required.

But in our human reality, separated from nature, what is considered a "good mom"? One who never yells, controls her emotions, handles her struggles behind closed doors, and protects her children from upset and difficulty.

Is that true? Is that a "good mom"? Does that protect our children or does it teach them to be nice, controlled, perfectionistic versions of themselves?

If we judge ourselves, constrain ourselves, and keep our pleasures and ambitions carefully within the acceptable lines, how will our children learn they can be big, messy, and create beyond the acceptable?

What if we, as Mothers, were willing to be all our energies, whatever is required, without shame, guilt, doubt, and regret? What if we allowed our children to be all the energy?

What if we did not have to judge anything as "wrong" but ask, "Is this what is required so the ecosystem of our family, of our lives, of my life that includes my children but is not just my children, can flourish?"

What future would that create?

Freyja is a warrior and a lover. She is the Mother of that which is beautiful and precious (the names of both her daughters mean "treasure"), and the intensity of her tears creates jewels. She does not hoard her potency but shares her magic for seeing and influencing the future. She shamelessly wears the gold necklace she secured with her sexualness. Half of those who die in battle find shelter in her fields. Now that Freyja has come to contribute to me, I will learn from her.

And I wonder, if you were also willing, Mama, to close your eyes, breathe into your deep, sexual, and creative core, allow the Goddess to touch you, be present with you, what are your gifts, as a warrior, a lover, a fertile source of magic, a fierceness, and bearer of treasures?

What Gift and Goddess are you?

MICHELLE NOBLE

ABOUT THE AUTHOR

Michelle Noble LMT, BF, CFMW has been a Licensed Massage Therapist and Craniosacral practitioner since 1997. She has been changing realities her whole life. In 2014, Michelle discovered the tools of *Access Consciousness*® and expanded her work with clients to include energy therapy and life coaching. The experience of becoming a mother of two giant beings in little bodies inspired her to create *The Calmer Mom Project*, in which she uses a unique combination of bodywork, verbal facilitation, coaching, questions, and magic to help parents trade perfectionism and anxiety for joy and peace of mind.

Michelle is a sought-after speaker, podcast guest, and host of *The Calmer Mom Podcast*. She is also a writer, singer, relentless possibility seeker, swears like a sailor, and loves cats, coffee, dark chocolate, her husband, and her kids (in no particular order!). You can visit Michelle to schedule a free chat, learn more or choose ease in pregnancy, birth, and beyond at www.CalmerMom.Solutions.

CHAPTER 4
FOR THE LOVE OF MAMA

By: **BONNIE MELITA**

I am in Love. Not the kind of love that gives you butterflies and makes you forget if your head is attached or not. Real love. The kind that is what we are truly made of. It's not even Agape. It's all-encompassing love. No. Encompassing sounds boxed in. The love I am talking about sets you free. Love where you know that time and space don't exist, love that comes from realizing the vastness of all that is.

Talk of love may bring to mind Venus but she is not the goddess I am currently enthralled with. While beauty and love have been major points of preoccupation for me, a different goddess has brought me this overwhelming sense of deep, grounded, mature love that makes me understand that I am unfettered by life. That goddess is Earth.

For me being in love came in an altogether unexpected way. I spent the last ten years or so taking care of my mom. For the last four, she was unable to walk on her own so I was her walker. I lifted her up as many times a day as she wanted. Then, with my arms under hers, I walked backward everywhere we went. Many have said they don't know how I did it, especially for so long. I say I don't know how I could have not done it and it wasn't long enough. I was committed to making sure she knew how much I loved her and how deserving she was for my whole life. Falling in love so deeply happened through my experience after she flew away with the angels.

Loving Mom was easy. She personified love to me and I aspired to be at least half of all I saw in her. The quintessential mama, guardian of the earth, and nurturer of all who came across her path.

Mom loved tirelessly and exemplified it constantly in many ways. She taught me to care for all life around me, to cook, sew, saw, and hammer because she wanted me to be able to take care of myself. She taught me to paint and hand-build pottery and took me to dance classes because she wanted me to know how to express myself.

Days were filled with observations of the beauty and magic in nature that surrounded us. Nights were no less adventure filled. She took me for moonlight bike rides followed by cookie baking with no light save the full moon shining through the ample kitchen window.

Sleep was often punctuated by her excited whispers waking me and urging me to come to the roof with her to see the meteor shower or lunar eclipse. If we weren't already sleeping on the roof on the mattress she had drug out earlier in anticipation of the upcoming celestial event!

My life has been a lesson in honoring the Earth. It was a top priority to Mom that I learn that respect and so it is interwoven into the very fiber of my being. To separate my mom and the earth is difficult. There was always so much love and respect for the Earth as Mother, a constant stewardship and caring for the earth in her every action that she was almost an extension of it. In reality, we all are but she embraced that and made a point of connecting to it in a million ways every day.

"I want to be thrown onto the compost pile", she would state emphatically. It was clearly important to my mom that she return to the earth as quickly as possible once she had exited stage left and no longer needed her body. My older siblings told her that was impossible. My small child mind couldn't fathom how it was possible. I quickly banished any thoughts about it. It brought up thoughts of dying and horrid visions invoked by a few trips to church in the deep South. The mere thought of life without my mom was awful enough without dwelling on details.

She was adamantly against being preserved and put into a fancy box. There was far too much that was unhealthy for the Earth. For a while, she considered cremation but decided it would take entirely too much fuel. Her belief, as she explained to me, was that if you try to burn green firewood it takes a whole lot of dry wood to make the green wood burn thus using more fuel. She said, "Obviously I won't be very dry when that time comes so I don't want to use all that fuel for cremation." She grew up in a house warmed with a fireplace, learned to cook on a wood stove for the family and farmhands at the age of eight, and had the task of building the fire for the schoolhouse at an early age. I respected her logic as sound based on her experience.

Being, whether in a body or out of one, was a fascinating phenomenon from her perspective. She never seemed to have any fear either way. She seemed to feel that we are either being birthed into the Earth or out of it.

Now that she has been birthed out of the earth I am left to reflect with deep gratitude at how she guided me to help her physicality merge gracefully into oneness with goddess Earth. This most recent journey with Mom may be the greatest lesson she has given me thus far. I anticipate there will be more lessons. I know she isn't finished.

On a late September evening shortly after dark Mom flew away with the angels. It surprised me even though I had been "being" prepared for it. Plenty of signs were there but somehow I didn't know.

I froze for a moment but the knowing set in. I began pouring my love into her. Yes, into the physical aspect of her, because that is where I was accustomed to directing my energy.

A few years ago I read someone's guide on what to do when someone passes to the other side. The main direction was to do nothing. That is what I did for a time. No thing.

I then announced that I was going to bathe her and wrap her in a clean sheet much to the horror of my companion who declared I would regret it and I would have to do it myself because he couldn't help. I did it. I knew innately it was not optional for me. As I washed her I talked to her and told her everything I was going to do before I did it. I expressed my gratitude to her for allowing me to take up residence in her body for nine months, for nearly bursting apart at the seams to allow my grand entrance into this world, for staying by my side, guiding me through life even when I didn't make the choices she wanted. I told her how much she always inspired me.

When I finished washing her I wrapped her in a new, clean white sheet and arranged the flowers my companion had picked for her earlier that day. Flowers in her hair as I had done all my life, particularly on special occasions, and more on her chest. I played a Jewish blessing for healing that a friend had played for her earlier that day on guitar. Afterward, we sang So Long, Farewell from The Sound Of Music. We are certain we heard her voice join in with us.

Then she urged me to make the call.

She had made it clear many times who was the first person I was to call when she left. He and his wife are like family. They were able to help tremendously.

I remembered Mom's stories of her childhood of family sitting with the person who had passed. There was no sending them away and hiding them somewhere so as not to face the situation. It seemed right to me that I should stay near her. The first time I walked back into her room I got a big surprise. Mom was always beautiful. Even when she flew away but I was not prepared for the beauty awaiting me when I returned. She had grown radiant. I don't know what this process is but I suspect it is not unique to her. Regardless I am grateful for the gift.

When the time came for her to leave I wanted to be present, to watch and accompany her to the vehicle waiting to carry her to the next step. My companion and our friends didn't agree and refused to let me. I didn't fight because I didn't want to push their buttons. They were emotional as well so I respectfully left well enough alone. It's a step I still wish I had done. It was crystal clear to me that I needed to be very hands-on. Mom wanted it and I needed it.

My companion and I went for a walk afterward. On this walk, I became keenly aware of Mom's presence and ability to still communicate clearly with me. She guided me through the next few days as I did the things that needed to be done.

Most of the words society uses to describe this part of life do not feel right to me so I allow myself to use the words that feel right. My relationship with Mom was so close, so different than most relationships, how could this part of our journey together be dictated by societal norms?

I can't bear to say the customary words to describe anything. Beginning with, "Mom flew away with the angels" and continuing with my point of view that we "planted her in a field on her beloved farm during a celebration". Not a celebration of life because that sounds depressing to me. Better than the f-word but depressing nevertheless.

I asked people not to wear black or depressing colors or buy florist flowers. Instead, if they wanted to bring flowers, pick them from their yards or wild by the roadside. Florist flowers and their florist shop odor, forms to hold them in place, ribbons and all manner of lifeless things that take forever to biodegrade simply didn't fit. As a result, the steady stream of loved ones walked across the field of dry, cut grasses on an early October afternoon wearing bright, happy colors. Red, yellow, and pink swirl in my memories as they came carrying gorgeous roses, black-eyed Susans, goldenrod, a grapevine wreath, and smiles. Yes, there were tears also but mostly born of joyous memories.

I had come earlier with those closest to me. Together we prepared for Mom's arrival. We found the perfect spot by using skills learned from BioGeometry which Mom and I studied together 10 years before. Thanks to a dear chosen family member using her expertise in this method the perfect spot turned out to be a power spot near mom's beloved garlic field which she had cultivated nearly all my life. Mother Earth has ley lines. Some emit energy that is helpful to humans and some emit detrimental energy. At the crossing of two helpful lines, a power spot is created that is particularly helpful and energetically powerful to our benefit.

I lay down on the spot to feel the energy of it. It was wonderful. So wonderful that I almost wanted to stay and it was clear that her heart needed to be placed exactly on the crossing. I lay there for a few moments feeling the support of the land and the glorious vastness of the sky as the sun warmed me, melting my tired body deeper into the earth that Mom's hands had given so much loving care to. The freshly mowed grasses cradled me and I was immediately transported back in time. Back to the smell and taste of the garden goodness she had grown there. Indian corn with squash and beans growing amongst it, tomatoes, field peas, potatoes, you name it. She walked barefoot making the rows with a hoe, I followed dropping seeds the prescribed distance apart. She would come back and cover them with rich, black dirt talking gently to them telling them to grow and produce so that we could enjoy their bounty. They listened and responded and I grew strong and healthy from this love that she poured into the Earth, seeds, and plants that grew. I was brought back from my reverie by the voices of my companions. They could feel the perfectness too. This corner of the Earth which she so lovingly tended was about to receive her.

We carefully marked the area and waited, listening to the wind in the top of the tall pines and birds chirping in the woods. I think they all knew and we're celebrating her return. She had been missed there.

The people who would prepare the space arrived and we showed them the area we had marked. In no time there was a hole in the belly of Mother Earth. Standing to the side, my companions holding my hands while watching the very reverent and respectful man inside doing his job, shovel in hand, I received a very strong message to get inside too. I expressed this aloud and my friend said, "Do it B".

I excused myself to the gentleman and asked if it would be possible. He smiled, lifted his hands, and carefully helped me down into the Earth. I began to press my feet gently into the sandy clay beneath my feet. I took a moment to admire the beautiful layers of rich soil and honor the fact that its obvious health was due to my mom's understanding of how to care for it. The years of mulching, rotating crops, and never, ever using pesticides, herbicides, or any other thing detrimental to Earth were obvious in the rich, beautiful life that was the soil upon which I had been raised and was now up to my chest in, bare feet pressed into it.

I took my time, making toe prints in every corner, squatting there, breathing my love into every inch of the space. Suddenly I knew what I must do. I must create a compost pile!

I called my companions who were keeping a respectful distance and a lovingly watchful eye on me. They were there in an instant. I asked them for goldenrod, dog fennel, some of Mom's garlic, autumn red blueberry branches, and anything else they could find that Mom loved. They brought all of these things and more, even a leaf from Happy, the fig tree mom talked to every day because she observed that Happy thrived when she had daily conversation. I placed them on the power spot where Mom's physical heart would be resting. On top of it all I placed a wire shape that our friend had made. It comes from the BioGeometry practice and resonates with the vibrations of all aspects of God. I then drew symbols in the earth that were special to Mom and me. Upon completion, I asked for help to climb out.

The act of hands-on preparing the space and washing my mom turned out to be two monumentally important acts in my process of falling in love and evolving into my life without mom in physicality. I am eternally grateful to her for guiding me to be involved. There are so many places in the process after someone passes in which we have the opportunity to pay someone to "deal with" the uncomfortable aspects that most of us don't want to think about let alone actually do. It turned out much better, for me at least, to be in the middle of everything I could.

I have always cried my eyes out anytime I see someone being lowered into the ground even if I don't know them. I didn't think I could watch Mom but when the time came I had zero emotional charge around it. I knew every inch had been filled with love and prepared for her. A beloved family member had even had the intuition to go to the beach and bring shells that we added. She knew Mom's deep love of walking on the beach, breathing the salt air, and gathering shells. The slight feeling I had experienced of incompleteness was gone with that addition. Clearly, she had called shells in to complete the preparation for her space. I was born near the ocean and lived near the ocean with my Mom when she flew away with the angels. Even the basket she was resting in had seaweed woven into it. I had chosen a different basket but heard her correcting me, saying she wanted the one with seaweed.

That is not a typo. She was in a basket. Her beautiful body was wrapped in a 100% silk blanket as she had expressly wanted and placed inside a woven basket. Fitting for an artist who worked with many mediums but largely basket making and pottery. For her to be in a woven basket and returned to the clay was only natural. I believe she is becoming her own environmental art as I am writing these words. Becoming the earth that she loved and respected so much.

She got precisely what she wanted when it came her time to be birthed out of the Earth. Her soul is flying about joyfully experiencing everything a newly birthed soul can experience as a newborn to the other side while her no longer necessary human body is becoming earth. A small part of the Earth that becomes a part of the greater whole. The composting process always changes organic matter into earth in a magical way that is nearly impossible to believe.

I am composting her lessons in my life. After all is said and done... I Am in love.

BONNIE MELITA

ABOUT THE AUTHOR

Bonnie is a constant student of life and all things spiritual. She was raised on an organic farm by a Mama who taught her to love the Earth and be a good steward of the land. Always fascinated with the possibilities of the human body, she spent much of her life studying dance and acting, becoming a leading actress and choreographer for a professional theatre company at 18 and the company's artistic director for the last two of her six years there.

She also worked in the film industry with a short stint as a stunt actress. She spent the last 22 years as a yoga instructor, teaching internationally with a yoga dance company. Delving into the healing arts, she is a certified BodyTalk Practitioner and Reiki Master and enjoys that aspect of human potential. Bonnie has spent the last ten years serving the Divine by caring for her beloved Mom. She is the author of two books: "Don't Panic! How To Use Yoga To Survive The College Experience" and the fully illustrated children's book, "The Good Witch Ella." She is currently in metamorphosis, moving into the next phase of her fascinating life on this planet with great excitement and anticipation.

CHAPTER 5
SELF-COMPASSION WITH QUAN YIN

By: **YVONNE IRENE ULLOA**

Finding Self-Compassion with Quan Yin

On March 15, 2022, I participated in a heart-healing session. The theme of that session was healing the Heart chakra. The session was part of a course on utilizing astrology and our natal charts to help heal trauma. My teacher looked at our natal charts and shared with us what she saw that was written in the stars. Then she introduced us to the guest healer who would support us that day by leading us through a Heart-healing session. I felt my heart open up and receive all the nourishment from that session.

When the session ended, the woman pulled a Goddess card for each of us. I wanted to get one of the Greek or Roman Goddesses since I loved learning about them as a young girl. I waited in anticipation for my turn. The Goddess card that I received was Quan Yin. I could see the women in the group smiling like they knew a secret, yet I was confused because I was unfamiliar with Quan Yin.

Who is Quan Yin?

That question plagued my mind after her Goddess card was pulled for me. I knew nothing about Quan Yin, yet curiosity led me to jot down her name. After the session, I did what everyone does when they want to look something up. I turned to Google. I typed Quan Yin into the search bar and immersed myself in the information.

Quan Yin is associated with compassion. Bringing in, creating, and developing more compassion for myself has been a big part of my healing journey. Reading about Quan Yin made me realize how fitting this Goddess card was for me. As I continued diving deeper to learn more about this Goddess, a memory from spring 2020 began to take center stage in my mind. A memory of when I held so much compassion for myself as I made a difficult decision that would take my life onto a different trajectory than I would have ever expected.

March 2020 began to mark the close of my second year as an elementary school counselor. I spent nine grueling years in college working on a master's degree in psychology and a dual master's degree in counseling specializing in marriage, family, and child counseling and school counseling. Those three years in my master's program were some of the most difficult years of my life. Stress, anxiety, confusion, and sadness constantly kept me company during those years.

Two secrets kept me in a state of constantly beating myself up during my master's program. First, I almost did not graduate from my master's program. The second was that I realized I no longer wanted to pursue a career as a therapist. My dream career entering the program was to become a licensed marriage and family therapist. The thought of pursuing that career path made me feel terrible. I spent most of my time not working on my thesis and beating myself up. I felt like I wasted the last three years for nothing.

Upon graduation, I packed up my life and moved from California to Washington. I would pursue a career as a school counselor instead of a marriage and family therapist. In Washington, I found myself working as a full-time elementary school counselor. This would mark the beginning of my three-year career as a school counselor.

My principal allowed me the creative freedom to design and implement my school counseling program, together with my associate principal, classroom teachers, and staff who supported me. The students on my caseload were easier to work with than my student caseload in my master's program. I adored my job during that first year. Creating the counseling program of my dreams and having an experience immediately post-graduation felt amazing.

I immediately renewed my contract without hesitation for another year. Once the second year began, I was excited to do it again. That is until I realized I would do the same year's first year repeatedly. I would teach the same curriculum and counseling lessons, facilitate groups, and tell the same jokes. I debated pursuing national boards, applied to mentor a school counseling intern, and for an educational doctorate. I needed somewhere to go. But all of that would buy me variety for three extra years. After that, I would repeat my first year over and over until I retired. That deeply frightened me. I was doing everything I could to push away those thoughts and continue to do the job that paid me well.

Those doubts and fears were easily pushed away from my mind due to a busy work schedule. But that crashed and burned me out in March 2020. In March 2020, schools were closed due to the pandemic. The moment that happened, I felt an immense relief that washed over me that I did not have to go to work. I had a small break from continuing to run on the hamster wheel that had slowly become my life. However, deep guilt surfaced when I realized I did not miss my job. Especially when I heard other teachers talk about how much they missed coming to work, seeing their students, the staff, and teaching.

At that moment, I realized I was unhappy with my career and could no longer play pretend. It felt like I was hit with cold water because I was out of options. I turned to school counseling when therapy no longer spoke to me as a career path. School counseling would be my lifelong career. But as school counseling no longer spoke to me, I had to admit I had nowhere to turn.

I knew I had to leave that career path behind, but I didn't know where to go if I left my backup career. My mind constantly swam in an ocean of negative thoughts. I had worked so hard in college for nine years. So many years that I had dedicated myself to studying. I felt like a failure for picking paths that no longer resonated or brought me fulfillment and joy. I felt like I had wasted my time and lost out on nine years of my life.

Criticizing and picking myself apart became my new hobby that summer of 2020. And it grew more as the beginning of the new school year began to approach. The new school year marked the beginning of my third year as a school counselor. I felt miserable waking up every morning and preparing for work. I continued beating myself up for being unable to push through and continue while school was held fully remote. This would continue until the schools fully reopened and brought back in-person learning in April.

In April 2021, I felt a deep dread come over me. The schools would be reopening fully, and I would need to return to work in person. When I returned to work, I felt even more miserable, and I continued to beat myself up for being unhappy. I felt like I had nothing to complain about or be unhappy about. I had job security, work benefits, and a wonderful salary, and the school I worked at was filled with amazing staff and students. Yet I was still miserable.

A deep sense of dread came over me when May rolled around. It signified that contract renewals would be coming up. The thought of my future and making decisions made me feel even worse and more miserable. I cried secretly through most of May - for my career and life.

One day I cried on my bedroom floor for what felt like hours. May was already halfway done. I still didn't know what I was going to do. The thought of letting down the sacrifices my parents made for me to have the life they always dreamed of for their daughter, be born in the United States, and study and pursue higher education made me feel sick. It felt like I would disrespect every sacrifice they made for me, and I would be disappointing them. I would no longer be the perfect daughter living the dream for her immigrant parents.

Telling my parents that I wanted to leave my job was impossible. The thought of telling my principal I would not renew my contract terrified me. In no way, shape, or form did I want to let him down along with the teachers and students. Instead, I would become the daughter that does not know what she wants and wastes her time. I carried so much guilt around desiring to leave because I was one of the few Latina staff members at my school and in my district. I wanted little girls like me to know they could pursue higher education and succeed. Leaving made me feel like I was telling those little girls I was a failure, not made for success.

In those moments of big tears, I felt a sense of compassion wash over me. I felt like I was receiving a warm hug and a message to show myself more love, understanding, and compassion. A compassion that is similar to Quan Yin's. Compassion for myself because I was growing, and I would outgrow parts of my life and identity in that process. At that moment, I decided that May 17 would be the day I told my principal I would not renew my contract. That weekend I would tell my parents the entire truth about my feelings and share my decision with them.

That week I felt like I was being cared for and watched by loving feminine energy. One that kept encouraging me to show compassion for myself. One that allowed me to make the most compassionate choice for my highest good. One that gave me the courage to put myself first after always putting others first. One that allowed me to experience freedom after I signed my resignation letter. One that gave me the strength to be honest with my parents about my career path.

It all started for me the moment that I showed compassion for myself. That energy was prominent on the day that I called my parents to tell them that I had resigned from my job. I will no longer be a school counselor in the fall of 2021. I was still determining where I would be and what I would do. All I knew was that I wanted to heal and feel good again.

The energy from the pulled Goddess card was when I first felt the energy of Quan Yin enter my life. That was the same energy I felt supporting me during the heart-healing session. She supported me through one of the biggest decisions of my life by reminding me to show myself the love and compassion I show others daily. The teachings and energy of Quan Yin have continued to support me on my journey throughout 2022.

The year 2022 has taken me down many paths I would have never expected back in 2018. I had the opportunity to spend the year traveling around Bali, Costa Rica, and Mexico. Diving deeper into spirituality and my healing journey became the focal points of my year. Toward the end of the year, the energy of Quan Yin came back into my life strongly. Throughout the year, I wanted to start my own spiritual business, share the lessons I have learned, and support women on their healing journeys. However, I kept telling myself that I could not do it, would not succeed, and that having my own spiritual business was a crazy dream.

In December, I found myself in Costa Rica attending a spiritual retreat. I was surrounded by amazing women that I found inspirational. I listened in rapture as the women shared their work. It was encouraging to hear from the women that ran spiritual businesses, but I also felt dread knowing that I would eventually be asked what I do for a living. I was embarrassed and afraid to admit that I had spent the entire year attempting to launch a business and feeling too scared to do it. I would try for a while and then quit. Each time I quit my business, I felt a deep sense of shame, and I would become my biggest critic. A repetitive cycle brought me into my darkest periods in that same year, 2022.

Quan Yin had been there with me through my darkest hours and gave me the courage to show compassion even when I felt I did not deserve it. Those feelings came through the strongest regarding my many failed business launch attempts. But for some reason, after each time that I would quit, I would feel the pull to try again. I felt an energy that encouraged me to try again and not be so hard on myself. That energy was prevalent and supported me through each conversation I had on that retreat, and I found myself sharing with the women that I would be launching a spiritual business in 2023. Quan Yin taught me that I must always hold myself with the same compassion in showing people in my life. I am just as worthy and deserving of that level of compassion for myself. This is a lesson and energy that I carry forward with me daily. I am forever grateful that this lesson and energy carry on with me as I work with clients through my spiritual business, Hermanas Healing.

YVONNE IRENE ULLOA

ABOUT THE AUTHOR

Yvonne Irene Ulloa is a spiritual coach. Assisting women reconnect with their feminine energy, bodies, and sexuality. She supports women in building their confidence and self-love and feels empowered. Yvonne teaches and guides women through her coaching practice, utilizing astrology, breath-work, EFT tapping, mindset coaching, psychology, and somatic healing to help her clients alchemize their dream lives. As a certified EFT tapping practitioner and an astrologer, she is also a love, sex, and relationship coach.

Yvonne Irene grew up in a Latino household in the Bay Area, traversing between two worlds. One was where Spanish was spoken at home with her parents and family, and another was where English was spoken with her peers and friends from school. She studied for eight years and holds a bachelor's degree in psychology and a master's degree in counseling. She specialized in Marriage, Family, and Child Counseling and School Counseling and spent six years working in the world of mental health before becoming a spiritual entrepreneur and world traveler.

Link to work or connect with Yvonne Irene:
IG Handle: @hermanashealing

CHAPTER 6
WHITE BUFFALO WOMAN

By: **MICHELE JOY**

My Soul Heard the Call of the Goddess White Buffalo Woman

Since childhood, I just knew... I knew there was something else beyond my human existence. I knew something of my true divine Essence, even if it was just a little. I knew I was a Soul.

That my physical vessel housed energy of an eternal nature. I also knew there was a reason I was here on Earth despite the dense frequency that challenged my sensitive, empath nature. Many of you will likely relate to a similar inner knowing. As frequency holders and energy transmuters, we feel the spark of our Soul, even if it is but a faint ember, yearning to ignite - we feel it from somewhere deep inside of us.

In childhood, many of us had experiences labeled "supernatural," Those experiences remain imprinted somehow, long past childhood, into the deep programming of our adult lives. For example, one of my so-called "supernatural" experiences at age five saw me waking up in the middle of the night to an enormous buffalo circling me on my bed. Whether this was the heavenly realm or whether I was completely awake, I'm unsure. I remember feeling awe of this great beast who gracefully ran in circles upon my body three times. I remember wondering how such a huge animal could run on me without causing physical pain. Then it disappeared, and I lay there bewildered about what had happened.

The next morning, I did not share my experience because I'd already learned that telling something like this to the adults in my house usually meant I wouldn't be believed and would feel silly. But this experience has imprinted on me to this very day.

Over the years, I have grown aware that the buffalo symbolizes a protective animal that has been a guardian. The frequency medicine of the buffalo provided grounding and foundation until I learned of the White Buffalo Woman and my connection to her frequency. Somehow this was connected to my Soul's mission.

The Buffalo energy has taught me determination and resilience, an inner strength that has enabled me to keep going where others might have given up. It has gifted me the ability to keep my feet grounded in Gaia while still exploring the higher realms. The frequency medicine of the buffalo has guided me to employ simple, practical, but powerful tools to explore my Soul wisdom. These same tools I use to guide others along their Soul path. Although I felt I was here for a reason, my childhood trauma and emotional wounding often blocked my trust in this knowledge.

You might relate, sister, to my struggle around oscillating between a nagging feeling that I was here for some higher purpose while also challenged by limiting beliefs of being unworthy. I struggled with chronic self-hatred, which meant for years, I made unhealthy lifestyle choices matching how I felt about myself. I chose to bury the depth of my emotional pain with myriad drugs and alcohol. I experimented widely with numerous types of drugs and high doses at times. Eventually, after ignoring my Soul's call for many years, I experienced a period of darkness as I experienced very deep grief. Finally, through this grief process, I heard the call to wake up and remember why I was here. This time I followed the call!

The Soul spark, the gentle but persistent knowing that the human experience was more like a dream than reality, expanded into a deeper realization. We are all uniquely blueprinted fractals, but paradoxically, we are also connected to all other Souls. And that something phenomenal and paradigm-changing was to take place in my lifetime. I started to remember the Ascension timeline in which frequency holders were here to anchor.

Once I was well on my journey back to remembering, a White Buffalo Woman reminded me of the specifics of my Soul mission. And it was a simple one, a simple loving mission. With my innate wisdom codes, frequency, and voice,

I was to activate the same healing and remembrance in others that they, too, are here to remember for a higher purpose. They, too, need to remember their divinity.

I have also connected with other Goddess frequencies along my journey, and I must add here that these frequencies are within us, not without us. If we feel connected to the frequency logos of a particular Goddess, it's because we hold a portion of that frequency logos. Most prominently, the other frequencies I feel within me are Isis and Mary Magdalene. Still, the White Buffalo Woman directly links me to my Soul path and purpose for the planetary Ascension we are now experiencing.

Each of you also holds your innate wisdom codes and frequencies that support your remembering. In turn, we move from our minds to our hearts, remembering to support Gaia and her planetary Ascension. Many believe their missions to be complex, allowing their minds to become entangled in figuring out what it could be, but mostly our missions are beautifully simple.

We are energetic frequency holders here to allow the ascension energies to flow through us, to anchor in our highest possible light. The best thing we can do for anyone and the Ascension or planetary consciousness shift is to shed our emotional woundedness, which blocks our evolution. Emotional wounded energy is a type of density within our field and body. The more density we shed, the more light photons we can hold, and the more our true divine wisdom codes are revealed to us.

White Buffalo Woman guides us to follow our hearts, to relinquish all fears of being what we came here to be. To be the truth of our Soul. She wants us to journey back to our hearts, to a point beyond time where we are in love with our being, and self-love fills our hearts and pours forth for all compassionately. She sends a message for us to transcend duality and return to Unity. There is no division between the masculine and the feminine, so we find a balance between the two frequencies. When we do, we attract our divine counterpart who has also returned to balance within themselves.

She constantly reminds me that I am an eternal beacon of light. She brings this message to me so I can activate this knowing in others. If you have a relationship with White Buffalo Woman, she might present you with a similar role, or she might be helping you with another aspect of your remembering altogether.

White Buffalo Woman is an aspect of Divine Feminine Christ, the Sophia Divine Mother consciousness. She asks us to remember that we are encoded with the divinity of love and encompass all, including Shadow, but this should be addressed, not ignored. Shadow work is to be used as a tool for mastery and reunification with our Christ Consciousness.

She tells me that the problem is many beings only remember their Shadow and have forgotten their light, so the Earth plane is full of Souls in pain. They bury their Shadow using false kinds of light in the form of addictions and avoidant behaviors to make themselves feel slightly better in the short term. Overall, these false kinds of light block their connection to their divinity.

Many don't remember their true divine Essence, their Soul light, or if they do, they don't trust this remembrance because of how dense the programming has been on the planet. We have been overlaid with a great density level, making it hard to trust our intuition and Soul wisdom. But through her frequency holders, White Buffalo Woman sends the message of faith and teaches us to cultivate inner peace and to trust our hearts for guidance. The divine knowing comes from the divine light within our hearts. Once you open the heart chakra and the higher heart chakra, you bring forth your true wisdom codes.

And then, my divine sisters of light, you will start to feel what you truly are – an incarnate being of divine light. A representation of the divine embodied in human form. Before your Soul chose to come here, you knew of the veiled human experience that you were to experience. You may have come in peacefully, full of confidence and courage for success in your mission, or you may have come in reluctantly, realizing the challenge before you. Either way, you still came, knowing so much but forgetting almost all for the journey back to your deeper core Soul mastery.

Now is the time to take up your throne of Self-Love, dear Queen, because, from the transcendence of your human trauma, you can shower all others with the same love you show yourself. Once you have felt your Essence, you will know no doubt nor fear because your once-wounded heart will open to receive and to give in equal portions. This is your natural organic state of being - these are the keys and codes your Soul holds.

My human aspect has traveled a long road to return to my divine feminine. This road is unique for all of us, but one thing is always the same, we must dissolve the overlays of the wounded feminine that masks the divine parts. We also hold wounded masculine aspects, and they need healing as well. Many women are operating in masculine aspects more than feminine ones, but this is changing; the awareness is raising. The journey is not over, of course, because, like you, I am a work in progress, yet my Soul knows Wholeness. As part of my healing journey, other women have been necessary to help shine my light even more because of my childhood; I held even deeper wounds with women than I did with men.

White Buffalo Woman reminds me and others that women and men are in harmony together -- the masculine and feminine balance provides peace and reverence to Great Creator Spirit.

As my healing abilities and wisdom codes expanded, White Buffalo Woman guided me with light language codes and ancient shamanic practices to help me move energy, run the light for my clients, and uncover their organic divine blueprints. To hold space while they heal compassionately, showing them how to heal with self-love and compassion for ALL.

We are here to be the bridge beyond those false matrix limitations. We are here as frequency holders and way-showers. White Buffalo Woman also guides us to bridge all gaps between masculine energy and feminine energy. Under her guidance, we set aside the "war of the sexes" matrix dynamics with a higher awareness that there is complementary sacredness to both the masculine and feminine attributes of which we all hold portions of both. The complement of these energies reflects the divine dance between the electron and the magnetic within our energy field. Knowing that we need each component, there is no advantage to competing for a starring role in the illusory stage of the 3D matrix.

The journey of the Soul is not meant to be complicated, but that doesn't mean it's easy. It takes commitment and courage to transcend our human wounds. So, when you need more comfort or courage, know you can call upon White Buffalo Woman's Divine Feminine Christ wisdom. She will hold space for the challenges that arise as you navigate the quantum leaps we are undergoing. She can offer support as you focus on your journey back to a heart-centered Christ Consciousness - the journey our Souls came here to make.

I leave you with White Buffalo Woman's message for Ascension in the following key points:

- Always follow the divine call of your Soul!
- Live your life cultivating peace and reverence for all that is!
- Do not fear or hide your divinity! This means rising above judgment from others - forgive them for they do not yet know, but there will be a timeline when they do.
- With love in your heart, be the bridge to the sacred union between the masculine and feminine!

Wishing you so much love and multidimensional blessings on your journey, sister,

Michele Joy

xoxo

MICHELE JOY

ABOUT THE AUTHOR

Michele Joy is an Energy/Sound Healer,
Mentor, Rebirthing Facilitator,
Breathwork Instructor, and Author.
She supports her clients to transcend their traumas
by releasing blocked energies and deepening their connection
to Spirit. Michele sees clients from

all over the world online and in-person locally.

Connect with Michele at:
www.sacred-healing-journeys.com

CHAPTER 7

HOLDING HANDS WITH DEATH

By: DIANA JYOTI, RN, MS

PART 1
Messages from Gaia

A couple of years ago, I opted for an abortion; it was one of the most healing experiences of my life. Yes, healing! When I was pregnant with each of my two daughters, I remember feeling like a Divine Goddess-- like Mother Gaia herself. Gaia is revered in Greek mythology and neopagan circles as the spiritual embodiment of the Earth—a Fertility Mother. I mostly dressed in soft, cotton, flowy dresses and wore a pendant of Gaia around my neck. I felt radiant. I felt a magnificent feminine force move through me. For the first time, I understood myself as an embodied channel of life force energy.

I have always been an energetically-sensitive person, and I have found that I can feel the consciousness of trees, people, and animals. When I was younger, it was a burden. Now it is what makes me an excellent professional hospice nurse, especially with patients who are nonverbal or close to transitioning. I can only explain it as listening for "downloads of knowing" from their energy fields to mine. In deep meditation, I would communicate with the consciousness of my unborn daughters. At the beginning of each of my pregnancies, I felt the consciousness of my two daughters' spirits around me but not inside me. I did not feel their energy vibration inside me until around 26 weeks. Yet, I could communicate with their essence outside of me as if it was right beside me. I'm not special in this. Every mother has the potential and capacity to communicate with the soul of their unborn baby if they have the will, desire, and open-mindedness.

Following my divorce, I became entangled in an unhealthy, three-year-on-again-off-again relationship with a man. His actions and words were inconsistent and unpredictable. I loved him and believed he was serious whenever he said he wanted to change and grow as a family with us. In February, he asked me to marry him. I said yes. In April, he disappeared from our lives again. In May, I found out I was pregnant at 40. I take full accountability for allowing myself and my children to stay in this relationship for so long.

I began communicating with the baby's consciousness in deep meditation when I learned I was pregnant. Again, I felt her energy around me, but not inside me. She told me she was female and wanted to be called Bernadette (Bernie for short). I explained to her that she had been conceived in love but that the father was no longer in the picture and had made it known he did not want responsibility for her. I told her that she would be born to a single mother without a local family for support. I told her it would be a high-risk pregnancy and birth for me at age 41 and that my two daughters needed me healthy and alive. I told her I was afraid I could not provide for her and my two older daughters financially or emotionally, considering the necessity of time off work, the cost of childcare, and only six weeks of paid maternity leave. I conveyed all of this to her in deep meditation. She conveyed my acceptance and willingness to come through a different mother. What is so beautiful is that I felt her understanding, compassion, and love move through me in waves of light. Even more than that, I felt us reciprocally healing one another in ways that can't be explained logically or scientifically.

In June of that year, nine weeks into the pregnancy, a girlfriend drove me to the clinic, where they gave me an Ativan and a local anesthetic. Within 15 minutes, the tiny clump of cells slid out. They asked me if I wanted to see it, and I chose yes. I did not want to delude myself or disassociate from reality. When I returned home, my female housemates held me in loving, compassionate arms. That night, I felt Bernie still around me. Her Spirit stayed around me for a week, conveying love, forgiveness, light, and joy. I grieved considerably, but I also felt reassured by her presence. I remember her conveying so much self-love and self-forgiveness to me that week. On the 7th day, I buried a talisman in her Spirit, prayed, and sang my appreciation to her Spirit, and then... she was gone. I have tears just thinking about it.

I haven't felt her since. Perhaps I will meet her again someday. But when I think of her, I feel so much love. It's as if Bernie filled me with a reservoir of unconditional love. I don't believe her soul/spirit died. I believe it went on to come through another mother.

The ex-fiancé and I have not spoken since then. Bernie gave me all the strength and discernment I needed to cut ties with him completely. I don't feel like a victim. I wish him well wherever he is. I learned so much about self-love, self-awareness, and healthy boundaries through this experience. I have done so much healing and self-growth work since then; my daughters (now teens) are thriving despite it. They, too, have learned discernment, forgiveness, and boundaries by watching me model self-love. They now know about abortion and my experience communicating with the baby's soul. They have both conveyed unconditional love and understanding for my choice. I am now engaged to be married to a man who is consistent in his commitment, love, and affection toward my daughters and me daily. This partnership feels loving, respectful, and honoring.

I know people will judge me as delusional or insensitive, but I know my truth. I share this as another perspective to consider. Take what you will, and leave what you will. Other women have had similar experiences but do not feel safe sharing them. Only decades ago, women were ostracized, persecuted, or even killed for sharing stories like this, and I suppose the collective fear still runs deep in the DNA of women. Those institutions no longer have power over us.

STORIES OF THE GODDESS

Here is a sharing from Christopher Chase I came across last month...

"In Japan, where I live, abortion is viewed differently. Here many people believe the spirits of the unborn have countless opportunities to incarnate, so if a mother chooses not to give birth, it doesn't mean the Spirit can't try again. The view that the unborn are spiritual beings that deserve our love and respect is shared, but women who have abortions are spiritual beings, and it is their right to choose. Even knowing this, many women will feel guilt or regret for their decision. So, suppose you go to cemeteries near temples. In that case, one often sees the status of Jizo Bodhisattvas with hats and scarves, some holding infants in their arms symbolizing infants who died and/or unborn spirits aborted or miscarried. Women and parents will come to grieve and pray, ask for forgiveness, and wish for the future happiness and return of the unborn Spirit that had wanted to incarnate. I've heard some Westerners say that the Japanese use abortion as a form of birth control. I don't think that's true at all. Most that I know take pregnancy very very seriously. To have an abortion is a tragedy. But it's also a part of the cosmic cycling of Spirit from life to life. In Eastern spiritual traditions, death is viewed differently, not as final. And life is deeply cherished. To some Westerners, this may seem paradoxical."

My own experience of abortion validates this belief system. I have come to understand death as a point on a continuum, with every soul having a unique and mysterious journey of multiple lifetimes and opportunities to incarnate. I have worked firsthand with hundreds of dying people as a hospice nurse. I've been privy to extraordinary and mystical experiences around death that have solidified my belief that death is a gateway to another realm. I've also read dozens of accounts of near-death experiences relating to the common phenomenon of emergence into bliss. Throughout all traditions, mythological Goddesses have exemplified divine compassion, mercy, understanding, and forgiveness. These are virtues I strive to exemplify in my life and profession. My experience of abortion taught me self-compassion, self-mercy, self-understanding, and self-forgiveness at a level I had not known before.

Simultaneously, Goddesses throughout all traditions have exemplified warrior-like boundaries and maintenance of balance and harmony through forces of creative destruction when needed. When necessary, Mother Earth can herald rude awakenings. Strong windstorms knock down decaying trees so healthy ones may thrive and grow taller. Sweeping forest fires stimulate new growth by clearing out smaller shrubbery, cleaning the forest floor of debris, opening the forest to sunlight, and nourishing the soil. Explosive volcanic eruptions eject sulfate-forming matter into clouds that block sunlight, thereby cooling the Earth. Floods can carry nutrient-rich sediments for vegetation and wildlife to thrive and serve to recharge the groundwater. These natural phenomena have been known to lead to human death and destruction. What we humans might deem inconvenient or exasperating, Goddess Gaia heralds as necessary for the planet's evolution in balance and harmony for all living beings. We cannot sit in a mother's judgment more than in the judgment of Gaia herself. To love a mother is to understand motherhood is not always roses and glory. Fertility does not equal obligation and self-sacrifice beyond one's capacity to cope. To support a mother is to trust her innate wisdom to feel into her unique life circumstances, to take stock of her goals and dreams for herself and her living children, and make the choices (sometimes difficult) that support her ability to balance all of it.

PART 2:
Messages from Tara

A thousand fireflies come together in vibrational affinity, and light more magnificent than any of them could shine individually is formed. And from that light, everything in the vicinity is illuminated. And from that conglomerate of illumination, everything becomes clear. There is nothing to fear. No shadows. No illusions. That is akin to what the Goddess offered me when she came to me and let me know of her affinity with me.

A year after my divorce, I struggled emotionally, mentally, and financially. I had many insecurities and self-doubts. One night I had a lucid dream in which I was standing in the back of a large auditorium filled with peaceful beings. There was a stage at the front of the auditorium. A strong divine presence encouraged me to look into a full-length mirror. When I gazed into it, I saw myself as a female dressed in an exquisite traditional feminine Eastern garb, wearing a golden crown and exotic necklace, with dark black hair stacked neatly on the top of my head in a bun. I appeared radiant, beautiful, and elegant. I felt light and unconditional love and bliss wash through my body. The divine presence was pointing toward the stage and urging me to take my place on the stage. I sensed the other beings in the auditorium were waiting for me to take the stage. I kept resisting, sensing that I wasn't ready. Over and over in the dream, I heard the word "Bodhisattva" reverberate through my body until I awoke chanting the word out loud.

I had never heard the word Bodhisattva before. I googled it and discovered that it is a term originating from the Buddhist tradition. One interpretation is "a person who is able to reach nirvana but delays doing so out of compassion to save suffering beings." In Buddhist culture, Bodhisattvas are often considered personifications of energy fields or vibrations that align to convey teachings and healings from the Great Spirit. Like fireflies gathering to illuminate the darkness, I have since understood the archetype of a Bodhisattva to be like vibrations of pure positivity and unconditional love aggregating to illuminate our hearts, minds, bodies, and spirits. I knew in my Heart that my mission was to find my place on that stage and become the model of compassion, loving-kindness, and non-attachment that I had had the bliss of experiencing in that dream. I also instinctively knew that it would not be an easy intellectual journey of self-wishing and hopeful thinking but rather a gritty, embodied adventure of self-awakening through trial and error, grief, loss, humility, and self-mastery.

I attended a women's circle a couple of months after that dream. A guest there had just returned from Northeastern India, where she had been leading workshops and performances of the Tara Dance. When she showed me a depiction of Tara on a tapestry, I knew immediately that that was the image of myself that I had seen in the mirror in my dream. I began to research Tara. Recognized as both a Bodhisattva and a Deity of the highest vibration, she is revered by practitioners of the Tibetan branch of Buddhism as the embodiment of perfected wisdom, loving-kindness, non-attachment, and universal compassion. She encompasses 21 divine feminine aspects, ranging from nurturer to fierce protector.

Since that dream, Tara has whispered to me in all areas of my life, especially in my work as a hospice nurse. A month after the start of the COVID pandemic, I was offered a job as a hospice nurse. I had just returned home from a vacation in Costa Rica, where I had participated in my first-ever sacred medicine ceremony. On the medicine journey, I was confronted with my fear of death. The confrontation with my mortality felt uncomfortable and agitating, but the moment I surrendered to acceptance around it, my journey turned to bliss and light. I felt the energy of the Bodhisattva move through me, and I was free. I believe that our ability to embrace the inevitability of death is vital to our ability to cherish life. I have witnessed that those who approach death with resistance often transition with more pain and agitation. Those who surrender gracefully to their death often transition with ease and peace. If we fear death, we fear life. If we fear life, we never take chances, challenge the status quo, wear our Hearts on our sleeves, love unconditionally, confront our shadows, make unique contributions, and never dare express our true selves. If we embrace death, we can have the courage to live to our highest potential because we understand life's finite nature and the preciousness of each moment as an opportunity to feel love and bliss. I now know that the medical journey was pivotal in my ability to work with dying people. My job as a hospice nurse requires that I encounter and navigate loss, grief, and frustration among patients, families, and caregivers—all day, every day. I have found I can hold a higher vibration of love and goodwill for them along their journeys because I don't have a fear of death to project into their experiences. I now intentionally practice embodying Tara daily, which allows me to hold more compassion, understanding, and equanimity for the dozens of people I encounter daily. I believe anyone can embody the Goddess through intention, will, and open-mindedness.

Furthermore, Tara is traditionally a fierce protector and defender of compassion and reason. One of the greatest lessons I have learned as a hospice nurse is when and where to set boundaries. Behind each door I walk through is an unknown, continually shifting soup of emotions, expectations, and situations to be managed. It takes courage and stamina. If I don't take time to replenish myself, or if my heart and body become numb from a lack of self-care and self-awareness, I cannot offer the balanced, grounded presence required to serve the highest good. The healthcare industry is mostly for-profit. If management is too overwhelmed, hurried, or overly concerned with administrative tasks and financial goals, they will likely forget their staff and clientele's human needs and feelings. In the last year, I have confronted middle- and upper management—risking my job and livelihood—to advocate for the needs of myself and others. We must all help reorient the healthcare industry to the heart of what matters.

I realized this past year that I have taken my place on that proverbial stage! With the love of the Bodhisattva moving through me, I have found greater harmony with my patients, friends, housemates, fiancé, children, and—most importantly—myself. Claiming my right to stand on that stage, I have a greater perspective on everything. Fully exposed at that stage, I can serve as a teacher when called upon to share my gifts. There is great responsibility in this, and also great reward. I approach my life and work with a personal mission to spread love, light, truth, compassion, and joy for the highest good. I now trust Spirit guides me in this and that Tara is behind me.

I believe we are all meant to be Bodhisattvas. We are conglomerates of eternal energetic life force energy having temporary focused desires and experiences in human form. We get to choose how we focus that consciousness in every passing moment. When we start to wake up to this realization, we can relax. Life becomes more fun and pleasurable. Even death becomes easier. Imagine the sheer power and magic of billions of incarnated Bodhisattvas coming together to illuminate this Earth! Imagine Mother Gaia celebrating this awakening!

May the blessings of the Goddess move through you more and more each day!

DIANA JYOTI

ABOUT THE AUTHOR

Diana Jyoti currently works full-time as a hospice nurse, where she loves helping people to transition with dignity and grace. Before that, she worked as a nutritionist, school nurse, breastfeeding consultant, and maternity nurse, helping people to transition into life. She currently offers life coaching and healing sessions from her office in Seattle, where she resides with her fiance and children. Diana has trained in Spiritual Response Therapy, intuitive energy, embodiment work, Constellation Therapy, and heart-centered hypnotherapy. www.dianajyoti.com

CHAPTER 8
GUIDANCE OF GODDESS SARASWATI

By: ANGELA ROGERS

**Living and Learning
My Saraswati Guru Guide**

I was exploring the woods near my home just after my birthday. This forest is the Earth's medicine bowl from the safety of the forest springs, a natural location for healing. It's the perfect beginning to my new ninth year.

It was early September, just as a new school year was starting. I turned nine in August. It was the perfect year for the perfect number, nine, for new beginnings. I was stepping from my early childhood into the next progression of this life:

the learning years. And who better to start that journey with than Goddess Saraswati? I still yearned to meet her.

The discoveries I would make in the next few years would move at the speed of light, taking so much in and learning from nature, books, and guides. My foundation starts with a connection to the Earth, water, and the forest. It moves through my body movement and, eventually, energy healing and purpose.

Finding Waters that Purify
―――――――――――

As I was exploring, I noticed a bubble of water would emerge out of nowhere every few seconds, but I thought it must have come from somewhere. As I stared in awe, little pressurized round water blobs came from the ground like they were coming off a factory line. The water factory, nonstop, in the moment producing, another blob of water, the continuous movement creating a sort of rhythm or frequency. Simply and consistently sparkling up from the Earth, an offering from the Mother. A small portal of water, a gift for her precious plants, animals, and trees, straight from the ground.

What had I discovered? What was this magical creation? I continued to stare at these continuous blobs of water being expelled from the Earth, staring in fascination and wanting to know where it was coming from. My nine-year-old mind didn't think it possible that this water could begin from nowhere, and why had I not noticed this before? It must be coming from somewhere up the hill. As I walked up the hill, the land was completely dry. Clearing away the layer of leaves on the forest floor, I pressed the palm of my hand into the dirt, and it came up again and again, completely dry. This must be magic, but no, it was nature. My mind had never considered where a stream might begin or how it began. Everything in life has a beginning, and how often do we consider what makes up an actual beginning? As I look back on this moment, Saraswati instilled in me a natural curiosity. Through the eyes of a child with hope and the splendor of Mother Earth, showing off one of her greatest resources, a natural artesian spring.

Was the Mother birthing this new stream of life to replenish all the living organisms in the area to drink from? What might be quenched by this new beginning? Why here? My mind was full of so many questions, yet no one was there to answer them. My Goddess guru guide was there. I didn't know it yet.

Finding the Bhagavad Gita

My stepfather arrived and moved in a short while later. When his things arrived, there was a milk crate of books. These were new interesting titles. They immediately captured my attention. I had wanted to get my hands on more books. Something interesting to sink my teeth into, to fall into the lost or hidden World that was somewhere or someone else's, anywhere but my own. A divorce and a new baby sister had disrupted the home. Her birth felt lovely and like a new beginning full of hope, but everything else felt very angry and sad and stung like the first sunburn of summer.

What was in that milk crate? I could see a large thick bright colored book. The jacket was full of pictures of blue people. Dressing in flowing garments and draped in gold. What mythical creatures had I come across? I ran over to look at it and was immediately told to mind my own business, and those were not my things. I'll have to check this out next time everyone else sleeps in. The wind was blown from my sails after being told no, but I knew deep in my heart I had found something special, and one simple "no" wouldn't keep me from exploring this fascinating crate further.

There was a new seating arrangement at the table. From my chair, I could specifically see the milk crate. I would stare at the crate knowing the answers must be in that one big book that looked so beautiful. So colorful, and somehow it felt like it was full of life. And the Bhagavad Gita was another book I had glimpsed when I dared to peek in the crate the other day. This book looked much smaller. There were no pictures, so what could it offer? A practicum guide had pictures, but they were in black and white. Boy, would I be surprised when I finally discovered their meaning?

Finally, after what felt like an agonizingly long time, the morning had come when everyone was at work or sleeping, and I had a moment to dig through the picture book. The images were glorious—beautiful full pages bursting with color. Images jumped off the page to create what I could tell was a story, though I didn't fully understand. There was an ending, and it felt like it ended in a positive place. Through the journey of Brahma, there was war, death, and tragedy. I wouldn't say I liked those pages much. But then, there was a birth and a feeling of happiness. When my little sister was born, I came to understand birth, or so I thought. I understood the meaning of it anyway.

The Story Depicts the Birth of Saraswati

Goddess Saraswati is the Hindu Goddess of knowledge, music, art, speech, wisdom, learning, science, and healing. She is depicted holding a book, a rosary, a water pot, and a Veena, the musical instrument. These symbols reveal her methods of teaching, healing, and carrying knowledge. As the story of her life goes, as mentioned in the Padma Purana, she was tasked with performing redemption for Vadava. To ensure this took place, it was said she merged into a Plaskma tree and then transformed into a river or purity, and the five channels flowed into the sea to create sacred waters. She became "the best of Mothers, rivers, and Goddesses."

Over time the etymology of her name has been translated for better understanding. Saraswati in Sanskrit is a fusion of "saras," meaning "pooling water" or "speech." And "vati" means "she who possesses." Thus, the "she who has ponds, lakes, and rivers" and sometimes "she who possesses speech." "One with plenty of water." These symbols of water, speech, and knowledge all collide to create a mythology around the purity of water and the possessor of knowledge. She has become more strongly known in the Vedas. Through the evolution of the works, she became a Goddess who embodies knowledge, arts, music, melody, muse, language, rhetoric, eloquence, creative work, and all creative efforts which flow and purify the Essence of Self. "Sara" is translated as "Essence," and "Sva" is translated as "Self." As follows, her name Saraswati translates to "She who helps realize the essence of self."

Kundalini Yoga and Light Energy Work

From these three books, the Bhagavad Gita, the story of the birth of Saraswati, and the Kundalini Yoga practicum guide, I was about to be hit with a birth of another kind. I was finding my inner strength where I would harness my energy and move into a practice I would cherish for life. One that would reside deep in my body and wrap around my soul. Protect me from the most difficult and painful things I would face in life and give me the platform I would stand on to learn, enjoy music, create knowledge, music, art, speech, wisdom, and learning—the melody of my life.

As Saraswati's birth from the mouth of Brahma was depicted in the book, I was moving through birth into developing a more significant curiosity and learning. During a tumultuous time, I was given my guide, my guru - Saraswati. She has stayed with me ever since, and I have grown closer and closer to her over the years.

It is from becoming the water that purifies to creating the speech that creates the knowledge of learning, arts, music, healing, and science. It's a virtual story of redemption. Gaining awareness that leads to the formation of our Self. One that many of us must go through to find the lightness in life. In sync with an artesian well continually pumping water from below the surface. Or an infinite loop where one side continually falls into the other. Mistakes are made, learning occurs, and redemption and healing are found. All the while, Saraswati is gently and firmly guiding the way. The Essence of oneself and our purpose for being here on this journey are revealed. Always seeking words through voice. Yearning for the written word. Working with those interested in pursuing a newer, more enlightened path has an openness.

For some, the resistance to energy work only allows them to see a different reality once they are ready. Those who choose it will go forward to listen through energy, voice, biomimicry, and body movement. Pushing or pulling energy through the body can reset so many versions of our cells. Science has a partial understanding of this phenomenon.

As a culture rooted in scientific pursuit, we lean towards being hesitant to define or describe ideas and things we can only partially explain in science. I believe in science, follow patterns, and see them in the treatments I've received and the benefits of life wellness I've harnessed through this work. Yet, we have many anecdotal experiences of significant shifts occurring through different energy modalities. Finding this struggle to create resistance as a teacher and a student has been a tumultuous ride.

For now, I still sit in the question of where this will take me. I don't have an answer, and ultimately I ask myself. Why do I need an answer? If this work helps, why not follow the breadcrumbs? Oddly enough, even if it is a placebo effect, scientific studies prove the placebo effect is real. Several modalities are popping up in our culture to align with all different people, gifting them paths into their future, so here we are, moving toward energy and light healing.

As Brahma meditated, a girl was born. He gave her the name Saraswati and duties. She was ordained to stay on the tip of everyone's tongue. She would dance abundantly on the tongues of learned people. Exist on Earth as a river; the third form would be to live in his person - Living on one's soul.

Listening to your inner voice for the answers that guide you. Acceptance and learning from your eloquent inner voice of melodic music. Ultimately, the speech will transform into knowledge as we gain more understanding. The art created to assist in healing is a powerful tool Saraswati uses. This loving, firm, and consistent reminder is coming through you and the deepest core of your soul. The speech we use can cleanse our thoughts and soul. It's being kind to oneself. The energy we can be to ask for our futures and desires will bring forth our abilities and gifts. Making this part of daily practice can bring an abundance of magnitude into your life.

The Evolution of Practices from the Beginning

An inclusive art, personal practice, yoga of awareness, flushing the energy through our system to support our life force. The energy is pulled through hands-on healing, a technology that has been around since the Egyptians, as depicted in the hieroglyphs. We strive for intelligence through sustainable and inspired practice, seeking empowerment and personal sovereignty, setting intention, connecting breath to movement. Guided by an evolving process using scientifically inspired inquiry and experimentation. If one attempts to consider themselves a novice, their practice will unfold organically and with a more robust potency. Saraswati inspires a beginner's mind and clears the path for learning and growth. We make mistakes, and she clears the path to move forward to a space of abundance in the new reality. Once we create by choosing to learn with her by our side and with a curious mindset, taking responsibility for ourselves, gaining knowledge, and being aware of our truth will take us places we never imagined you could go. Find your niche in the healing arts. Seek. Love. Heal.

We choose the energies we align with to bring those choices to us, from understanding our re-births, past experiences, and how we want to create our life. These are difficult for us to recognize in our path, like obstacles in front of us. That disconnect is going on to stifle our growth. Get on your mat, get some energy healing, and find clarity around your questions about the gifts you want to receive in this lifetime. These struggles are timeless, a hazing we go through to attain greater heights and successes. Are we often too focused on success to miss the small things that matter and give great abundance? The creativity of the Self and from your person is like artesian wells coming from the Earth.

Saraw=swati translates to
"She who helps realize the essence of self" She has a gentle, loving energy with which she guides us with a firm and loving hand, pushing each of us to learn and grow, to become our full potential.

Saraswati has a gentle, loving energy with which she

guides us with a firm and loving hand, pushing each of us to learn and grow, to become our full potential.

We learn how to feel again and learn how to learn again and again. No teacher is more significant than one's own experience. Yet, Saraswati is with me, with us, if you choose. She teaches us that we've always had our power. It's been there all along. Reinforcing that all life has equal value if only we ask and demand it.

Each person, their voice, and their presence in this time matters. And, if we ask her to help remove obstacles to help us gain knowledge, she will surely gratify us with comfort around the gift of learning, knowledge, and wisdom in what we create and, thus, the melody of our lives. A tune we know as our own that fills us with great accomplishment and confidence.

The gift - our gifts, Saraswati's Goddess gift is to encourage all of us to Be the muse of our own life. Look for your Goddess. What is showing up in your life? Be curious. Be mindful. Just Be.

"Presenting to you, Sarasvatī,
these oblations with reverence (may we receive from you affluence); be gratified by our praise and may we, being retained in your dearest felicity, ever recline upon you, as on a sheltering tree." - Rigveda, 7.95.5

Angela Rogers

ABOUT THE AUTHOR

Angela is a highly skilled energy worker with love for spiritual growth and a steadfast commitment to her clients. Her unique approach blends ancient wisdom with modern techniques to empower individuals to unlock their full potential and live their best lives.

As an intuitive energy worker, Angela specializes in identifying and releasing energetic blockages and realigning chakras. Her gentle yet powerful touch helps clients achieve balance and harmony in their minds, body, and spirit.

With a deep understanding of the mind-body-spirit connection, Angela's holistic approach is grounded in compassion and a genuine desire to help others achieve happiness and fulfillment. Her clients rave about her ability to identify and overcome the root causes of their energetic imbalances, leaving them renewed and empowered.

If you're seeking a transformational experience that will help you tap into your inner potential, Angela is the energy worker for you. Get ready to unleash your full power and live the life of your dreams!

To Find Angela Contact:
arogers8758@gmail.com

CHAPTER 9
ANOINTING OILS OF THE GODDESS

By: PATRICIA WALD-HOPKINS

Opening Blessing

There is a sacredness in ordinariness. To be of this world fully embodied as a human yet a holy being of benevolent light. Service to others in the healing arts is an act of holiness. The holy anointing oils from the plant kingdom bring the individual into balance with their divinity and humanity on Mother Earth. The one that anoints is a conduit of embodied grace.

Priestess of Anointing Oils of the Goddess

I FELL in Love with aromatherapy about 14 years ago while training to become a massage therapist in Santa Fe, New Mexico. One of my favorite teachers at this school shared her gift of aromatherapy with our class, and since then, I have been blending essential oils for physical, emotional, and spiritual needs. My approach is both intuitive and scientific. I lead with intuition and use my studies of the biochemical characteristics of oils and the human body to fine-tune my blends. It is very natural for me to create blends for myself and my clients. I have a very deep remembrance in my body of blending and anointing. I believe it is a gift that originated with past lives as a priestess in the temples of Isis and with Mary Magdalene.

People experience cellular remembrances such as a deja vu, but they don't know how to explain why they have a deep connection to a person, place, or thing that feels beyond this lifetime. Many in my generation, including myself, came into this lifetime having forgotten our soul essence and soul path. It isn't until we are triggered by a traumatic or miraculous event that we fully activate and remember our soul essence and path. Some say this is planned ahead of time when we set up our soul experience for this lifetime. That is what happened to me. I was 36 years old before I began to remember my gift as a priestess of oils. And it wasn't for another decade or so that I truly deepened my archetypal work with the oils that now include many of the faces and aspects of the Goddess. Before my awakening, I had studied as a scientist and focused on the body's biochemistry and how substances interact with the body positively or negatively, resulting in improved or deteriorated health, respectively. I was onto something here, but not in the higher dimensional realms of alchemy. My science background no longer leads my work, but it has become a sound foundation for creating my blends in the third dimension by working with the physical body each of us chooses to incarnate into in this lifetime. My soul knew I needed this scientific foundation to ground higher consciousness alchemical blending of essential oils into my sacred feminine business. So I am grateful for my life's journey merging science with the metaphysical, allowing me to walk the path of a modern mystic.

The Goddess Isis began working with me and my sacred gift of anointing with oils more deeply when I began working with the wisdom of the Akashic Records and the Gene Keys, both benevolent tools of higher consciousness. While working in my Akashic Records, I could speak to the Goddess Isis and download the archetypes she wanted me to share with the world. She showed me the archetypal codes of all the Goddesses I hold, and I could manifest them using digital art, essential oils, and the Gene Keys for each anointing perfume. The Gene Keys serve as the holographic blueprint of the Goddess frequencies of my anointing perfumes. What a gift to receive from the Goddess in this way! I even created my Infinite Self oracle card deck that includes these many Goddess archetypes as part of the higher self wisdom in the oracle deck.

The Goddess Isis guided me through my calling to share these archetypes in my work with clients to support them in embodying the various frequencies of the Goddess that they need most at any point in their evolutionary journey.

The Goddess Isis also guided me to use them in my Butterfly Healing Method™ sessions to activate the codes of the Goddess. At the same time, I work with my clients on the healing table along with the other vibrational healing techniques with sound, crystals, and light language. Isis guided me to use the digital art I created for each Goddess archetype to create sacred altar cards that list the powers of the essential oils plus any crystal allies and a written transmission from the Akashic Records. The art 'itself' is a powerful transmission from Isis as received through my Akashic Records. Each Goddess archetype has an accompanying crystal or stone, sound/tone, and light language frequency.

Goddess Anointing Oils

Over the last decade, I have intuited blends to tap into the frequency of other realms, including the devic, the cosmic, the angelic, and the divine feminine realms. Usually, I receive a transmission that I ground into the third dimension as a digital art collage. Then the individual essential oils reveal themselves to me for that archetypal frequency, but other times the oils reveal themselves to me, and then the art manifests! I have created over 50 plus sacred and magical blends available upon request from my alchemical boutique. I paired them with crystals and wrote and recorded high-frequency Akashic Wisdom transmissions and digital art. The first Goddess blend I created was the Alchemical Priestess, the

Butterfly Medicine Woman, that seeded the Butterfly Healing Method™ I created through my work with vibrational medicines over the last 14 years. Below is the 12 Goddess blends list with a brief description of the oils plus Akashic Records contemplation.

- Divine Mother (Goddess of Love) - Unconditional Love & Peace

Take solace in the lap of the Divine Mother. Let her embrace you with the sun's warmth and the oak tree's steadiness. She radiates the essences of turmeric, rose, frankincense, myrrh, neroli & jasmine.

- Dragon Queen (Sovereign Being) - Divine Presence

She offers you the essence of sovereignty. Fully embrace your power and value your uniqueness. Her golden dragon medicine is to be a harmonic being of Love and peace for the cosmos. Find support from the essences of geranium, pink pepper, cypress, galbanum & cistus.

- Ecstatic Queen (Goddess of Passion) - Liberation

She calls upon you to speak the truth that frees women from the bondage of conformity, mediocrity, and compromise. Speak with your voice, choices, and how you love yourself. She radiates the essences of ylang-ylang, jasmine, neroli, rose & sandalwood.

- Iney (Priestess of the Peacocks) - Benevolent Free Spirit

She offers you the radiance of self-assurance, joy, beauty, and kindness as you open your heart to receive the higher frequencies to live in the benevolent service of the collective. She radiates the essences of sweet orange, patchouli, hyssop, fennel, blue yarrow & davana.

- LuLu (Priestess of Abundant Light) - Embodiment of Abundance

She guides you into the fields of abundant, golden delight where mana falls from heaven, nourishing every cell in your body to experience abundant life on earth. She radiates the essences of tagetes, patchouli, fennel, hyssop & neroli.

- Mary Magdalene (Voice of Freedom) - Spiritual Revolution

She is the record holder of the ancient secrets of life. She grants the creation codes of harmony and peace to bring a spiritual revolution in the darkest places. She radiates the essences of turmeric, rose, frankincense, myrrh, sandalwood & cacao.

- Metamorphic I (Alchemical Priestess) - Magic & Metamorphosis

Your soul is awakening. The ego lets go of control of your life. The veils fall. The magical light of your soul is being revealed. You are supported in your alchemical metamorphosis by her. She radiates the essences of petitgrain, black pepper, hyssop & rose.

- Metamorphic II (Alchemical Priestess) - Love, Magic & Metamorphosis

Your soul has awakened. The veils have fallen. Your soul is brightly shining with Love. You have up-leveled. She rejoices that your alchemical metamorphosis is complete. She radiates the essences of petitgrain, pink pepper, hyssop & rose.

- NuNu (Priestess of Earthly Richness & Resources) - Embodiment of Prosperity

She offers an elixir of ecstatic bliss, Earthly richness, and resources for a bounteous life. She radiates the essences of tagetes, patchouli, cacao, clove & cinnamon. Be filled with the deep, sensual nature of Gaia. Be in harmony with the web of life.

- Orchid Queen (Enlightened Being) - Joy, Love & Compassion

She offers you the frequency of joyful compassion. Be gentle with yourself as you evolve. She supports you to be a powerful beacon of ecstatic delight in service of Divine Love. She radiates the essences of litsea, Roman chamomile, bergamot & lime.

- Soja Ne (Water Goddess) - Joy, Love & Vitality

She offers you the frequencies of deep passion and Love for your body and humanity. She invites you to access your sensuality to increase vitality through ecstatic states of bliss. Find support from essential oils of basil, spearmint, blue tansy & ylang-ylang.

- Tula (High Priestess of the Light Sanctuaries) - Sanctity, Truth, Love & Light

She offers the frequency of pure white light sanctuary to protect you from negativity so you can discern the most loving and heart-centered choices to create more light for the world. Find support from essential essences of black spruce, frankincense, rose & angelica.

Vision for the Future

The Goddess Isis continues to guide me in expanding my work with oils. I have been guided to create a journey of Divine Indulgence that takes the journeyer through the

Goddess archetypes using the Akashic Records plus Gene Key contemplations, art, and sacred movement to support women to fully embody the frequency of that Goddess archetype represented by the anointing perfumes. I plan to host virtual and live Goddess retreats. I have been guided to prepare an initiatory path for sacred feminine leaders to continue to work with these oils in their lives and with their clients if they have a sacred feminine business amenable to using them. The Goddess anointing perfumes will be incorporated into the Butterfly Healing Method™ certification.

Butterfly Healing Method™

I mentor clients while holding them in the cosmic Mother harmony frequency that bathes and saturates their cells with this energy allowing a shift in their biochemistry to be open to experience harmony on earth. I use my Butterfly Healing Method ™ to do this work. This method includes various Vibrational Therapies, Akashic Record Guidance, and Multidimensional Oracle Card Activations. Vibrational Therapies include sound healing, light language activations, crystal therapy, energy healing, chakra balancing, Reiki, aromatherapy, craniosacral therapy, and sacred movement. Higher self-wisdom and identifying which chakras need healing and balancing to fully activate and embody a client's unique multidimensional blueprint. Multidimensional Oracle Card Activations are based on a codex of light that I developed through my art and contemplations to assist others in recognizing the key aspects of their multidimensional self, which includes cosmic, elemental, and higher self wisdom. I also use the codex to fully identify what karmic healing or chakra healing is required in your multidimensional power in this lifetime. The codex is a 55-card oracle deck published and available to my clients and the public. Akashic Records Guidance is soul-level work to illuminate blocks to a client's soul mission, clear them, and implement new ways of being and doing through my inspired life coaching. I also weave in Gene Keys Guidance as a sacred map of higher consciousness to support a client's process and basic human design and astrology elements.

Closing Blessing

Never deny the simple need to receive grace and be open to your multidimensional higher self and your sovereignty as a sacred feminine leader in human form. This is the greatest service you can offer the world now and for all generations to come on Mother Earth. Blessed be the one that shares the light of grace with others in the sacred act of anointing oils. These blessings reach 400 years and beyond, shifting our human DNA to express the Goddess within. Blessed be the ones that walk in Her footsteps. Thank you for receiving this transmission.

PATRICIA WALD-HOPKINS

ABOUT THE AUTHOR

Patricia Wald-Hopkins is a Modern Mystic, Infinite Self Catalyst, and Soul Liberation Guide for those ready to break free from old paradigm limitations and awaken to their Infinite Self and lead the life they are DIVINELY designed to live. She is an Akashic Records Wisdom Guide and creator of the Butterfly Healing Method™ that supports her clients to

embody their Infinite Self. She is a Gene Keys Ambassador & Guide and co-founder of the School of Light Collective. She is a collaborative author in several best-selling books, including the chapter Butterfly Medicine Healing, in the book Energy Healing & Soul Medicine, and author of the chapter Stardust Blood: Codes for Harmony on Earth, in the book Awakening Starseeds: Dreaming Into The Future, Volume 3. She is also the creator of the Infinite Self Oracle Card deck and creator and host of the Divinely Inspired Woman podcast.
Www.patriciawaldhopkins.com

CHAPTER 10
EMBODYING THE GODDESS WITHIN

By: **AMORITA MUGNO**

"You've Always Been Held."
-The Goddess

To the beautiful, radiant, and Divine Goddess reading this sentence...Thank you for being here. Thank you for incarnating on Earth during this time. Thank you for showing up. Thank you for being you. Thank you for picking up this book and taking the time and space to read these sacred words as you soak in these messages.

As you read the unique stories shared within this sacred transcript, you are gently invited to activate the Goddess that lives within you. You are choosing to expand your Soul's consciousness and contribute to the collective Divine Feminine frequency on the planet and beyond. You are actively participating in grounding Heaven here on Earth now. Seriously... right now, as you read these words. Take it all in. Breathe it all in. Embrace it all. You came here for this and are here for a significant reason, dear one. By being here and opening yourself up to receive the divinity embedded within this book, you are choosing to learn more about the Goddess in all of her forms, ground in your sovereignty, and tap into the great Goddess within YOU! She is ready to emerge once again. She is ready to reclaim her unique gifts and operate in absolute Divine Essence. She is ready to embrace her journey and ground in her purpose. She is ready to hold you through whatever experiences life gifts you with. She sees you fully, honors you wholly and supports you always and in ALL ways. She guides you when you ask her to (and allow her to); most of all, she loves you infinitely and unconditionally. She is limitless. She is kind, expressed through the form of inspired action. She is the gift of GRACE and compassion. She is intuitive, wise, and receptive. She is soft and gentle yet strong, bold, and wild. She is the energy and frequency of unconditional love embodied. She is what our World needs most-- right now. She is the Goddess. She is the Divine Feminine. She Is Within Each Of Us, and She Lives Within YOU!

The Divine Feminine's ever-lasting Essence is a direct channel for the infinite divine wisdom we all have the power to tap into. If we choose to, of course. That's right. We have a choice. Always. Even right now, at this very moment, as you read these words, you may choose. You may choose if this is another book you read, soak in and then proceed with life the way you always had. OR...In this very present moment, you may let this be a transformative point and powerful shift in living, writing, and co-creating your Goddess story. Your story is also in the process of being written, and it is important not only to you but also to the entire collective.

Sweet love, would you believe me if I told you that you truly have the ability and power to co-create the life you've always dreamed of living? A life that is Divinely Aligned with your heart's most true desires and your greatest passions? A life filled with bliss, passion, peace, happiness, joy, freedom, and love of all forms? A life of creating and sharing your unique Goddess story and embodying the Divine Goddess that lives within you, leaving a lasting, loving, and positive impact in the World? Would you believe me if I told you that YOU are LOVE in HUMAN FORM?! Do you believe it? Well, it's true.

This is what the Goddess asks you to remember now. You are worthy of it all, sweet being. Your desires have been placed in your heart for a reason. There is a greater purpose behind your most natural and intuitive desires. Maybe you don't believe it just yet, and that's OK... but I hope that by the end of this chapter or this book, you will. As I write and channel this particular chapter, I wish for you first to know that I am writing directly from my heart space to yours. I intend that by sharing aspects of my story & how I have worked closely with the Goddess, you take whatever you need and leave the rest as it may be for someone else, or perhaps even for you at a different point in your journey. May this sacred text find you in your perfect Divine Timing whenever you need it most within your journey.

I could sense someone "out there" rooting for me ever since I was a little girl. Little did I know, it was my own Highest Self and Inner Goddess holding me, guiding me, rooting for me, and unconditionally loving me all along. She was within me the whole time, and I am here to remind you that she is also within you. Throughout our Soul's journey and sacred experience on Earth, seeking our worth through things or people outside ourselves is easy. We are somewhat conditioned to do this without even realizing it. It can feel easy to "lose ourselves" in the experience of life. We play many different roles throughout our lives, especially as women. We may play the role of a daughter, perhaps a sister, a student, an employee, a boss, a friend, a lover, a partner, an aunt, a niece, a granddaughter, a grandmother, and so on. Our roles are forever shifting. Some roles we may graduate from, some may expand or shift, and others may fall away as our journey unfolds and takes its divine course. This is a lot, sweet Soul. This is why it is most important we come back home to our TRUE selves, WHO we are to the CORE.

This is our most important role here on Earth. To reconnect with our inner Goddess. To tap into our divinity and remember that our infinite Essence is exactly that... infinite. We are here to remember this divinity – even in adversity, uncertainty, or pain. This is why we are here. To expand our Soul's consciousness. To reconnect with our Soul's purpose. To remember WHY we incarnated here in the first place. This has been my focus and intention over the last several years, and it is what I am most grateful and inspired to share with every beautiful Soul I have the pleasure of connecting with. My mission and purpose here on Earth are to remind

OTHERS of their sacred divinity. To remind them of their unique purpose. To lovingly guide them home to the Goddess/God already within them. I am a big believer in showing the way through our thoughts, words, and actions, all being in divine alignment for our Highest Good and the Highest Good of all, as I strongly believe and know that we are all a part of a collective. It is so much bigger than just our personal incarnation. It's about raising the entire collective consciousness as a whole. But to do this, it must start within us. We must first connect with our inner Goddess and remember that she has been within us all along. When we can recommit ourselves to tapping into and remembering our source of divinity, which is connected to the source of divinity itself, then we naturally become a lighthouse for others to remember they're free to do the same. This is the ripple effect. When we ground in our sovereignty and tap into our unique gifts, we remind those around us that they have the power to do the same in their unique way. This is finding the Goddess within. My life shifted for the greater good when I reconnected with my inner Divine Feminine and started to embrace, understand and embody her fully. This was when I thought my work with the Goddess TRULY began, but the reality is, she's been within me all along. It was simply a matter of remembering, trusting, and allowing her to shine the remarkable and unique light she came here to express and share with the World. This is why we're here. This is the power of the Goddess.

The Goddess can be found in every living thing; she reminds us everything is living. She is God's Consciousness embodied in unconditional love, acceptance, patience, and grace. The Divine Feminine is the force that is gentle enough to embrace and nurture us as if we were newborn babies and powerful enough to transcend us into the next phase of our Soul's journey with peace and ease. She is the portal that births all creation into being. The Goddess will save our World; to save our World, we must first save ourselves.

My journey of saving myself began in childhood. Being born into what some may call a 'dysfunctional' family, I've always had a gift of heightened awareness and intuition that has carried and supported me significantly throughout my journey.

As far back as I can recall, I remember vividly looking around at the situation I was born into and thinking, "Wow, this is some pretty messed up stuff happening here." It seemed clear how things would unfold if they continued as they were; unfortunately, that is exactly what happened. I witnessed my Mother keep herself stuck in a continuous loop of suffering. I watched her make choices I knew would end up killing her one day; unfortunately, I took the brunt of her frustrations and pain. My Mother appeared unable to do the inner work due to her own personal issues & ever-growing alcoholism. Out of all of my five siblings, I was the one who wasn't afraid to tell her directly that the way she was living was detrimental to herself and those around her. Some of my earliest memories consisted of me trying to express that her actions were wrong. This didn't go well for me. The more I would call my mom out, the more she would resent me, and her verbal abuse escalated into a physical outburst that gave me no choice but to "run away" to live with my dad at age 13. I knew I didn't deserve what she projected onto me, and after that moment, I decided it was best for me to leave and cut her out of my life. I didn't speak to her for years, as I needed time and space to heal. Her condition worsened, and every time she ended up in the hospital, I was the one to visit her. Although I didn't speak to her, it didn't mean I loved her any less. My relationship with my Mother was the driving force of my journey of inner work, and I had a lot of healing to do.

One thing I know about inner work is that it is SO worth it! Even as a child, I KNEW I was experiencing what I was here for a reason. I believe my strong desire to dive so deep internally and heal the generational traumas passed on throughout my family lineage, and possibly even throughout other lifetimes, was inspired by watching my Mother get stuck in her suffering. I never wanted to make anyone else feel how my Mother made me feel, so I committed my life to dive deep within. I committed to healing, growing, expanding, and sharing these tools I've found with those around me. I knew someday I would speak of my story, which would be someone else's saving grace.

Although my Mother's love was the definition of conditional, as it was solely based on whether I pleased her (or not), there was a greater love holding me throughout my journey: the unconditional love of the Goddess. The Goddess has shown up for me in multiple forms throughout my entire journey.

I have always been naturally drawn to the Goddess archetypes and energies. The Goddess archetype I first resonated with was the Warrior/Huntress archetype. My whole life, I have been an ambitious go-getter. When I set my mind to something, it was a sure thing I would get it one way or another, and I wouldn't stop until I did. I am still this way, and I am truly grateful. Embodying this archetype saved me and kept me inspired throughout my childhood. It allowed me to pursue a greater life than the one I was born into. I know the Warrior Goddess's energy to be intentional, courageous, strong, wise, intelligent, fierce, ambitious, and bold. The Goddess that first showed herself to me through this Archetype is Athena, the first Goddess I intuitively knew. When I thought of a Goddess, I thought of Athena. She felt the most familiar to me. Many consider Athena the Goddess of Wisdom. She is known to appear with an owl, signifying her infinite wisdom and great connection to the Divine. Athena is a warrior, but what I love the most about her is that she uses her wit and intelligence rather than physical force.

Another Goddess I greatly connect with that embodies the warrior and huntress archetype is Diana. Diana is said to be a Roman Goddess equated with the Greek Goddess Artemis. I connected with Diana through my first oracle deck, The Goddess Guidance Oracle deck by Doreen Virtue. Her card represented "Focused Intention," and she was seen holding a silver bow and arrow. I shoot a recurve bow, so the card instantly resonated with me. Diana reminds me that when I set my intention and stay focused, I will surely make my mark. I am so grateful for this divination tool because it has allowed me to learn more about different forms of Goddesses and directly channel their wisdom.

Working with various Goddesses has shown me that the Goddess truly is incarnated in many forms. Some Goddesses I work closely with are Kuan Yin (Quan Yin), Yamanja, Lakshmi, Saraswati, and Danu. When I first began working with these Goddesses, I would see them as 'greater' than myself. I unintentionally put them on a pedestal and considered myself inferior. One day in meditation, all of the Goddesses I had ever worked with appeared. They were all there in their greatness, almost as if they were lined up. They took my hand and placed me 'in line' with them, telling me I was a Goddess myself, just as powerful as they are, but in my unique way. They gently reminded me that everything I need is within me, so I am inspired to share this message with you, Queen! It can be easy to consider ourselves inferior or to seek our worth outside ourselves, but the Goddess lovingly reminds us that we are sovereign and worthy of our heart's most true desires. Knowing we are worthy of receiving is a belief in itself that takes practice to integrate. One of my greatest desires has always been to come into harmonious union with my divine love, my King. I have always been a lover and romantic at heart. Throughout committing myself to my self-love and self-worth journey for years, I distinctly remember a moment when I felt I was 'ready' for my King to enter my life. I meditated with my guides and angels and asked, "How do I call in my Divine Masculine?!"

Surprisingly, the answer dropped almost immediately, and I heard, "Come Into Your Divine Feminine." The clarity that followed these words resonated with every Essence of my entire being. After hearing this and sitting with it for as long as needed, I wondered 'how' I would do that and got curious about what that looked/felt like. Shortly after the meditation, I opened my Instagram app on my phone. The FIRST thing that popped up was an ad for "The Divine Feminine Archetypes Challenge" hosted By Melissa Wells –

someone I had never heard of until this point of my journey. "You're doing it. Sign up." My Higher Self spoke to me.

Without hesitation, I signed up for the challenge, which started the following day. I knew this was a crucial step in coming into my Divine Feminine, and I love how the Universe responded to my inquiry almost immediately. Now it was up to me to listen and take inspired action, and Wowza, I am so glad I did. I committed myself to the 7-Day challenge and showed up fully with an open heart. Out of thousands of women participating in the challenge worldwide, I received the final prize, a full scholarship to Mel's exclusive membership, 'The Goddess Collective.' This opportunity changed my entire life. Upon receiving the scholarship, I gifted myself with a tattoo of two flowers connected by one root with the words "Divine Timing." This is such a loving reminder that our deepest desires are in our hearts for a reason, and sometimes the first step to moving toward our heart's desires is to ASK, get quiet, and create space for the answers to flow naturally. So Dearest Goddess, Sometimes, we begin by searching for something we think we want and find something even greater, or maybe we realize that we never needed to search at all. May we all continue to trust that everything we need is available to us, and may we recognize, once again, the infinite gift that's been within us all along.

Amorita Mugno

ABOUT THE AUTHOR

As a Divinely Guided student of life, **Amorita** is humbled and honored to be of service to the collective through her unique purpose and mission. Considering herself a passionate advocate for growth, healing, and reclaiming personal sovereignty, Amorita holds the pure and loving intention to remain in divine alignment with her highest and most authentic Self while inspiring others to do the same, wherever they are on their path. Attaining various certifications and embodying impactful lessons throughout her journey, Amorita shares her gifts and intuitive wisdom through a grounded and heart-centered space. Her multi-passionate offerings include creating and hosting Inner-WorkShops; speaking, writing, yoga, 1:1 coaching, group coaching, intuitive channeling through oracle readings, energetic healing, Holy Fire® Reiki, and guided meditations. Amorita speaks freely on her podcast, The Shrink Yourself Podcast©, as she encourages all to "Spread the Love, Be the Peace, Bring the Light."

www.amoritaspurpose.com
Instagram: @AmoritasPurpose

CHAPTER II
SUPER KALI

By: LEAH SONARIA EMMOTT

Part 1: Invocation

My mouth was full of candy hearts when I had the truth bomb of all truth bombs drop in on me.

"You remember that photoshoot we did last year inside that old abandoned church in the forest?" Musashi said, handing me a pre-emptive joint to soften the impact.

My mind returned to the roofless concrete structure overtaken by vines nestled in the middle of the lush Hawaiian rainforest, adorned with spraypainted Goddesses of all varieties. Some were pretty, some were enchanting, and some rose out of the vegetation naked and blue-wielding machetes hungry for blood.

"Yeah, that was such a perfect spot to shoot my collection of Goddess shirts. Why do you ask?" I replied, noting the coy Buddha smile on my favorite local photographer's face.

"Well... you're not going to like what I'm about to say, but hey, this kush don't lie. That was Kali's temple, you know. She was front and center on those walls. Remember, we shot that Super Kali slogan shirt in there? How did it go again?"

"Super Kali Fiery Mystic Shakti Inner Goddess," I responded, lilting the words playfully off my tongue to the tune of the Mary Poppins classic.

"I don't think it was just some funny slogan, Leah. I think it was actually an... invocation. That explains all the big shifts you've been going through lately: the breakup, the downsizing of your clothing company, the stuff with your family. I think you summoned her.... in a big way. You super sized her, even! It was a bestseller, right? You broadcast that mantra all over the world. That'll get her attention, alright."

My jaw dropped, revealing a tongue appropriately stained red.

"What? No..no..no.. you're just playin' with me - there's no way I summoned her. She's just a character, an archetype, a myth. It was just a silly slogan I made up. It doesn't mean anything."

"Words are powerful, dude. Spirit's always listening. She's a feisty one, that Kali - likes to use her machete to hack your life to pieces when you're not paying attention. But remember, she's all about death and rebirth. She'll only cut away anything you're not."

STORIES OF THE GODDESS

Part 2: Destruction

Kali has an interesting backstory. One version of her origin myth says that she started out as a tongue for hire - Agni, the fire god's tongue, to be exact - tasked with licking up drops of Raktabija's blood (which means blood seed) on the battlefield to stop each drop from spawning into a new little demon. Kali did such a good job eradicating those pesky little monsters that she graduated to deity status, still batshit crazy and bloodthirsty, but now complete with a near-naked blue/black body adorned with the season's hottest trend in body parts. She became a household name, developing a refined palette for all flavors of ego, and eventually evolved into her more benevolent form as Dark Mother.

My tongue, on the other hand, wasn't quite as virtuous. It had a tendency to get me into trouble - the kind of trouble that had me waking up swimming in someone else's bedsheets, hoping it would save me from drowning in the red with my failing company and equally faltering near marriage. From the outside looking in, my life seemed great: a solid long-term partnership, a new cute little character home, a popular clothing brand, staff, and yearly excursions involving getting lei'd in paradise. But on the inside, my heart was breaking into a million pieces. I was bleeding money, had no creativity left, and could barely get out of bed most days.

The scarlet letter written on me wasn't exactly a badge I wanted to wear. I knew the pain of adultery all too well. When I was 14, my Mother cheated on my father with a horrible man, and it tore my family apart. I'd been cheated on before by an ex-boyfriend, and it shattered my whole world. You'd think I would have known better, but somehow my actions left me oscillating between the agonizingly blissful realms of Shame and Shambhala.

My 'lust' interest wasn't exactly what you would call boyfriend material. Not even boy toy material. Just some hipster dude from an old friend circle I happened to be re-acquainted with at a rock show one night. It's as if Kali was out bushwhacking with her machete out of boredom one day and stumbled upon a tasty treat. "You'll do."

Something had overtaken me. Despite having what seemed like a healthy sex life, I was insatiable, reckless, and so caught up in the throes of ecstasy that I somehow found a mullet attractive. It wasn't really the sex I craved, though. It was something else: I wanted to feel alive again. The Kundalini serpents were ready to rise, and there was no stopping them from piercing through the veils of mediocrity with a current of liberation so strong I swear I was about to come out the other side as a boy wizard. In the grip of such high voltage, the only path to mercy was utter and complete surrender. With each moment of embodied rapture, Kali led me deeper and deeper into the bardos of my inner world until I found myself at the threshold of an unsuspecting portal: the front door of my Mother's house.

Part 3: Preservation

After we split, I decided to move back home to live with my immigrant Mother and her less-than-pleasant live-in handyman boyfriend of 20 years. I won't go into the details of our past, but let's just say that entering into their world was like stepping onto a minefield.

A few things to note about my mom: she's a Vietnam war refugee, is gorgeous as hell (i.e., never ages), and is usually found at the bottom of a large pot making enough food to feed a small village. She's from the 'Tiger Mom' school of parenting, a lovingly ferocious rearing style that produces top-notch over-achievers, perfectionists, and prize-winning people pleasers.

As soon as I entered the kitchen, I was greeted by a couple of characters that lived in the grain on the original varnished plywood cabinets of my childhood: an owl on one panel and an old Chinese-looking man with a long beard on another. They were the closest thing to modern art we had. Well, if you don't count all the accumulated sauce splashes from every meal my Mother's ever made.

When my sister and I were kids, my mom would recruit us to help her make a big batch of Vietnamese spring rolls. She'd source the finest ingredients - fresh crab, pork, wood ear mushrooms, vermicelli noodles, onions, and grated carrots. We were tasked with soaking the rice paper and passing them to her as she rolled each one. The timing had to be perfect - ten seconds, and they'd crack; fifteen, and it was mush. There wasn't anything much worse than handing a mom a sticky, soggy sheet. That shit could get you disowned in this family.

As I walked in the door, she came in from the living room to greet me, the faint sound of reality TV drifting in behind her. I could see the concern on her face under her homemade honey-papaya-mulberry-leaf mask.

"What are you doing here with all your stuff?' she asked as if I'd just crossed the border illegally.

My chest caved, triggering an uncomfortable twinge in my low back, no doubt resulting from being my 'own' sweatshop worker printing shirts for months. I was hoping to sneak in without being seen.

"We...we broke up. It's over between us. I had to leave. There's nowhere else for me to go. Can I live here for a while?'

"What about your house? All the money you spent? You've been together for eleven years already. How you gonna have kids now?" she scolded.

"I know, Mom. I can't really explain it. I just need somewhere to land so I can figure this out."

Her face had the same expression as the first time I handed her a piece of soggy rice paper. It was the kind of a silent disappointment that could cut you deeper than a Chinese meat cleaver. I wanted to cry but couldn't. As grateful as I was to have a place to go, I couldn't deny that despite my best efforts, I still had not lived up to her expectations.

"Okay, take your old room upstairs," she said, weary and disappointed.

It wasn't exactly the welcome I wanted, but at least I had a place to land to figure my shit out. I let out a sigh of relief and thanked her with a big hug. As I collected my things, she motioned towards the large pot simmering on the stove. "You want something to eat?"

Despite her hard exterior, her cooking comforted me in

ways words could not. Food was her love language. As I sat there devouring a piping hot bowl of delicious kohlrabi watercress soup, I swear the old bearded man on the cabinet door gave me a wink. "Welcome home, kid," he said.

I went upstairs with my things. The emotions would have carried me away had it not been for the enormous amount of stuff staring straight at me when I entered the bedroom. Over the years, the room I shared with my sister as a kid had become a modern-day archeological site, a dumping ground for all sorts of random junk.

I carved out a path and began my excavation. Buried deep in one of the boxes was a real gem: a copy of my band's very first CD, aptly called "Seeing Red." I pulled out the liner notes and unfolded the inside spread. Four sets of eyes on a red background stared back at me on the cover. We were an all-girl teenage rock group, and I played drums. The four of us looked fierce, wearing red lipstick and ready to smash the patriarchy with anthems that screamed, "Don't try to cause me hurt you're dirt."

With a bright red mop, I'm rocking my dad's vintage Rolling Stones tee with the sleeves rolled up - a nod to the classic rock that raised us. It was the only hand-me-down my sister and I ever fought over, accumulating holes like bedside notches (she slayed on guitar too). I later learned that the iconic Rolling Stones logo was based on a depiction of Kali's mouth, so it turns out that every time I stuck my tongue out in teen-punk angst, it was her signature ferocity that I was embodying. No wonder I hit those drumskins so hard my fingers bled.

I'm not sure if it was sorrow or nostalgia, but reminiscing about those times left me in a puddle of tears.

Knock, knock, knock. My mom popped her head in.

"Everything okay in here?"

"Yeah, I'm fine. Just going through some stuff right now," I said, sniffling and smearing snot on my sleeve.

She walked over towards me.

"I know. Breaking up is hard. But look at the bright side, at least now you have a nice place to do your yoga." She walked over to the full-length double-wide mirror in her tight yoga outfit (my designs, of course) and busted out a sassy hip move followed by a bold bicep flex.

"How'd you get so fit, mom?"

"Mom always finds a way to stay healthy. You wanna know my secret?" She moved some boxes out of the way and pulled a hula hoop from the closet. She stepped inside and launched it around her waist, moving with the grace of a swirling supernova. Across her face was a playful smile I had not seen in ages.

"Here, you try."

I stepped in, brought it up to my waist, and gave it a whirl, my hips chasing to catch the edge. I could barely make three revolutions before it fell to the ground. Hooping wasn't exactly my forte.

"It's so easy, though! You follow it around too much. Just move your hip side to side, not in a circle. Let it come to you. Make it more like dancing."

I tried again, allowing my hips to find a steady rocking rhythm. To my surprise, it stayed up! I reveled in my accomplishment until she took the hoop back and decided to one-up me by adding some Latin-inspired dance steps and belly-dance arm movements to the mix.

"Oh, so now you have to show off?"

"This is how Mom stays young. Keep practicing, and you'll be as good as me one day," she said cheekily, handing it back to me to have another go before heading downstairs.

I carved a path over to the wall-sized mirror and stood in front of it. At thirty-three, the grey hairs were on the offensive, popping up like an army of the risen dead. The cumulative effect of going through the wringer over the past few months began to set in on my face, with those dreaded 'elevens' creasing ever deeper with every eyebrow furl. Yet, there was something that felt alive in me, not the aforementioned kind of aliveness ushered in by lusty nights but an aliveness imbued with a wholly different essence. It was a feminine force, a stirring in my pelvic bowl that felt foreign and familiar. Like that hoop, a spiral path led me to the next stage of my evolution. The terrain was smoothing out, awakening an intuitive, sensual, and primal remembrance. My hips began to move in figure eights and circles. A feeling of deep self-love began to radiate from my heart, and as I looked at my reflection, Kali stared back at me with ancient eyes.

Part 4: Liberation

If I know anything about Kali, it's that she doesn't waste any time. After all, she is time (in fact, her name translates to 'black time'), and as a master chronomancer, she's efficient as fuck. Within less than a month, I had a competitor interested in buying my company, was dancing on the regular, and was finally beginning to feel good about life.

I still felt like a horrible biz mom for putting my baby up for adoption, but I couldn't resist the force that kept pulling me toward those double doors of emancipation, bringing me closer to the twin pillars of a much-needed giant pause. Unlike the creases between my eyebrows, it was a set of elevens I was happy to see.

Amidst the chaos of sloggin' it solo for six months, I managed to carve out some time to attend a breathwork training recommended by a friend, mostly to see if the simple act of breathing could lighten my heart enough to clear the guilt that still weighed me down like dark matter.

The session began with hypnotic, primal rhythms. Drums, wood flutes, and didgeridoos escorted me to my inner hinterlands. I tried to employ the mouth-only breath pattern, attempting to seamlessly ripple the breath from my belly up into my heart, which was about as flexible as a slab of concrete.

After about fifteen minutes, my hands began to tingle. Kali's essence washed through me, irrigating my system with a subtle bliss. It was a gentle pulsation, imbued with healing energy that traveled over the leylines of my body, inviting new levels of sensation with each passing breath. I could feel my roots connect deeper with the Earth, deeper with my ancestry, deeper with the Mother within me.

Then, out of nowhere, a woman near me let out a bone-chilling "FUCK YOU!!!" and I immediately launched into an uncontrollable coughing fit. Barely able to gulp an inhale, a deep surge of energy rushed up from my sacrum and burst out from my lungs into an ugly, guttural howl. My tongue stretched out over my lips, and I arched my chest wildly, my eyes rolling back into my head.

Kali was back. Her ancient rage bubbled up from the darkest depths, my mouth becoming her loudspeaker, filling the room with more earth-shattering cries. Millennia of oppression were being purified through me.

My body, electric and hot, prepared for another surge while my mind, unable to fathom how any of this was happening, sat back and watched in disbelief. As I opened my mouth, a dark, sticky energy spewed out of me like a stream of oil gushing up from the depths of the Earth. I went into full exorcist mode, my tongue pinned to my chin and my jaw pried wide open like a roaring lion as if I was opening a portal to another world.

I thought a demon flew out of me, struggling to catch my breath.

My release set off a cascade of cries around me. A woman near me writhed as if she was giving birth, her feet pressing into her facilitator's stomach so hard she nearly threw him across the room.

Just when I thought I'd gone completely mad, a female facilitator came over and whispered into my ear: "Return to your womb, sister, return to your womb." Immediately, I was back in the room my sister and I shared as kids - our womb room. It was tidy and welcoming, a sanctuary of safety. My body buzzed with soft power.

The gentle beating of a drum steadied the field. Great Mother's heartbeat was guiding us back home. As the energy settled, I felt a reassuring hand holding mine, still tingling and twitching. I'm not sure if it was spirit or human (my eyes refused to open), but her grip pulled me out of my body and out to another plane. It's there that I met God. She and I became one, unified in the sanctum of our glowing red hearts.

I found out later from one of the facilitators that I had stopped breathing for about two minutes, turning a nice shade of Kali blue. Everyone always told me I looked like my Mother.

LEAH SONARIA EMMOTT

ABOUT THE AUTHOR

Leah Sonaria Emmott, aka Flow Priestess, is a transformational guide, quantum activator, and ceremonial spaceholder. After selling her 7 figure yoga clothing business in 2019, she embarked on an intensive healing journey that led her to discover her purpose as a spiritual mentor and ceremonialist.

Through dance, breathwork, plant medicines, tantra, and flow arts, she activated her flow consciousness and creatrix power. Her deep study and practice of the divine feminine mysteries unlocked her medicine as a light language channeler and sonic alchemist.

As a devoted Priestess of Isis and Hathor, she works with Egyptian alchemy to support visionary creatives to activate their highest soul blueprints and birth their creative legacies with flow and ease. She is currently finishing her first memoir, Super Kali.

www.flowpriestess.com

CHAPTER 12
THE HUGGING GODDESS

By: **SELMA HARTWELL**

Amma The Hugging Earth Goddess

After giving me the gift of her hug, Amma saw right through me. "You are a lion in sheep's clothing," she told me.

Amma was born with divine abilities to share. Her miraculous hugs help clear obstacles in people's lives, allowing them to move forward.

Before hearing of Amma, My Goddess experience unfolded with 8 New Mexico sistars and New Moon ceremonies created with our beloved Elder, Peggy Coyne, who shared her Art Historian expertise of Goddess teachings with an impish Irish expression and her Goddess ways of living that were devoted to sharing abundance for community philanthropy. Peggy showed us how to practice ancient Goddess ways for each of us. For 18 years, each month's created intentions seeded at our New moon ceremony designed to be fulfilled by the full moon. We gathered for an evening of fun, food, kids, and 25 women. Oh my gosh, our favorite times together were such a pleasure-making Goddesses of magical clay! We were inspired by our Goddesses emerging from the sparkling clay containing the shimmering Mica element that connects to the heart, and our Goddess brilliance shined outwardly! Next, our magical community of The Sacred Feminine attracted a female Shaman named Ohkie Forest, whose original core of eight women practiced traditional ceremonies for eight years, building a sweat lodge by harvesting the willows to bend and tie into a supportive shelter that housed our prayer ceremonies. Many tribal ways, like forming a medicine wheel for more prayers and so much more. It became a deep dive into our healing while exploring other realms and developing our intuition further.

 I first met Amma through Rose, my admired voice coach I worked with for eight years, so hearing about Amma coming to Santa Fe in a few days was intriguing. Instantly drawn to see Amma, I quickly connected with a friend in Santa Fe to have a playdate for our girls while I saw Amma. My excitement grew to "check her out" as the plans flowed effortlessly.

 Friday comes at last. The winding road led to a sparse forest where I parked, and a short walk led me to the largest tent I had ever seen. Indian-style carpets covered the massive floor, covered by hundreds of closely seated people singing interactive chants, and all eyes were fixed on the stage, awaiting Amma's entrance. The notable drone of the harmonium fills the air, echoing Mantras being sung. The crowd rustles, quieting as the music softens and the anticipation is tangible...Amma is coming!

My senses heightened, and suddenly I knew Amma was behind me! My head instinctively turned! I had one clear thought: "Oh my God, I'm in the presence of a Christ-like being!" I was grateful to be sitting near her unexpected entry. Amma continued down the fresh path of people that opened before her as she passed. Amma's water blessing was about to start, followed by people lined up for a hug from her. I was grateful to enjoy the ceremony for a while, then I felt a nudge to leave, sensing it was time to gather my daughter for our planned journey home.

My friend opens her door, and I hear myself say: "Can we spend the night? "My jaw dropped as I looked around, shocked, wondering who said that, as I recognized a strong urge to see Amma the next day. We were graciously welcomed to stay the night. I realized it was my first blessing by this Earth Goddess-even without a hug and I wondered how the magic of Amma had me return to her. The next morning...

We enter the rearranged tent, bleachers surrounding the room, leaving space for Amma at its center, ready to give hugs. I witnessed firsthand the immense love that Amma pours into every person she hugs, and I marvel at how she can do this for so many people for so many hours. How is that possible? The level of love was unimaginable - a sight to behold as tears streamed freely from my eyes. I couldn't look away and cried for 5 hours at that loving sight as if true compassion cleansed my soul to let the love seep in! I experienced limitless love in the space of the Divine once more. I realized my second healing had happened just by observing Amma giving hugs until my heart was purified. Even waiting in the long line to be hugged by her was worthwhile!

A memory returned of my trauma at four years old. Being in a Divine Love immersion that I knew as God was the immediate gift. It set consoled on the path to receiving many more gifts of sensitivity throughout my life. I was left with "claircognizance" - the gift of knowledge that connected me to the gift of my Shamanic lineage. I had much development to go before fully recognizing those three gifts. Surrendering to the work that took to unfold was natural, and listening for the timing and seeing the purpose played out is the reason for discovering a great mentor. The transmissions nurtured my path by providing a new level of healing that I would pass on to help mothers learn self-care, heal themselves and their families, and impact the world. It is my passion in life and my most rewarding work!

Each time the Mantra music welled up, I welled up too! My turn for Amma's embrace came before I knew it, and I was finally with her. Devotees position me to make room for Amma's full embrace. That brief hug was a transformational initiation when Amma applied Sandalwood paste to my 3rd eye. I suddenly feel multiple electrical energy surges coursing through my body! My eyes are closed, and I'm lost in timelessness. While on my knees, I feel both arms extended outwardly as my body sways forward and pulls back with each surge! I vibrated: Voom...Voom...Voom...Voom-I lost count!

When my body stills, I burst into tears as I opened my eyes. I felt humbled and newly me in my reconnection to blissful peace and felt replenished by this profound blessing. Amma's interpreter then asked me to choose a Goddess for my Mantra from Amma to repeat daily 108x. I chose Kali! That's when Amma gave me the message: "You are a Lion in sheep's clothing!" I'm reminded of my strength because of my triple fixed-triple power of my Leo Sun, Scorpio Rising, and Aquarius Moon, plus being born at the magical hour of noon on the day Mother Mary assumed her body. Each profound connection enhances every other magical gift I have received since childhood. I know now that Amma meant for me to see how I hide my power. It is unintentional when I hide - a habit to catch more quickly as a lifetime practice of releasing those moments because we are only human and not perfect. I learned that the more willingly I honor myself and relentlessly value the Goddess part of me being connected to the heavens, the more I remember ways I have always been connected.

The name" Amma" means Mother in many parts of the world! From a young age, As a Holy Mother of India, Amma continually surprised everyone with her empathic skills. By transmuting negative energy without taking on their burdens, she demonstrates we can all learn to let things pass through us without holding onto them, especially beginning as empathic healers and developing beyond the original experiences. One year, I was grateful to receive an extended hug from Amma. I felt so lucky and beamed like a favorite child while Amma kept holding me with one arm as she waved around her other arm directing her devotees' in Seva (service), helping provide the best care for her "guests." I loved every minute of her embrace that showed me all Goddesses have much to manage in everyday living, including families, children, talents, careers, and friends that make up our whole life. We draw upon the Goddess's high frequency and do our best to handle what may come in service to living authentically to who we truly say we are! My commitment to the feminine includes my stand that Motherhood is honored as a source of world peace so that Moms learn the ease of self-care for healthier families reflecting in better world health.

I'm 71 years young, focused on living well to 115! My healing skills came to me with relentless faith and a heavenly connection. Sacred Communion came at age eight - also the number for magic, I kneeled at the altar for photos afterward, and my gaze locked with Mother Mary. I'm transported, sensing a tangible heat sensation between us, and I am graced with Mother Divine Essence to become my signature healing. With a candid click, Mom captures the moment during that incredible experience. Weeks later, I had forgotten about it when Mom showed me the photo with the light beam between us! I remembered the magic that happened on that doubly sacred day!

The magical connection continues growing by listening intently to the knowledge and speaking the guided ways to serve, heal, and help others. Taking action immediately after a message comes through always brings better results than imagined.

I cherish the memories of my encounters with Amma and her profound impact on my life. Amma's story is a testament to the power of empathic and grounded healing and releasing quickly. Her remarkable hugs have transformed countless lives and helped people discover their potential. Amma gives millions of extraordinary hugs; maybe one will be for you!

RADHAA NILIA

THE GODDESS EXPRESS

LOOK PAST YOUR MESS
TO THE GODDESS EXPRESS

GODDESS ARISES FROM WITHIN
THE SPIRIT OF YOU THAT HAS ALWAYS BEEN
AND EVER SHALT BE

BE THE GODDESS YOU ARE
FOR YOU'VE COME SO FAR
HAVING RISEN THE BAR

IN FRONT OF YOU

GIVE IN
TO YOURSELF
STEP UP!
STEP IN!
TO THE SELF
THAT IS EVER YOU

SHINING FROM THE INSIDE OUT
SHINE BRIGHTLY LIGHT FAIRY,

LIGHTLY

INWARDLY BLESSED

STORIES OF THE GODDESS

GRACEFULLY PRESSED
TRULY EXPRESSED!

YOU OF THE SKIES
THAT NEVER DIES
SOMETIMES HIDDEN
IN DISGUISE

GODDESS ARISES FROM WITHIN
THE SPIRIT OF YOU THAT HAS ALWAYS BEEN
AND EVER SHALT BE...

DELIGHTFUL

GO THROUGH THE SETBACKS
MEANT FOR QUERY
THEN LISTEN AND
YOU ARE LESS THE WORRY

THE WINGS OF PRAYER
YOU GET TO BORROW
EACH TIME YOU GRATEFULLY
RELINQUISH SORROW

LISTEN AND FLEE,
NOT AWAY -BUT NEAR GLEE

FREE YOUR SOUL AND JUST BE...

RADHAA NILIA

GODDESS ARISES FROM WITHIN
THE SPIRIT OF YOU THAT HAS ALWAYS BEEN
AND EVER SHALL BE

— Selma Harwell

SELMA HARTWELL

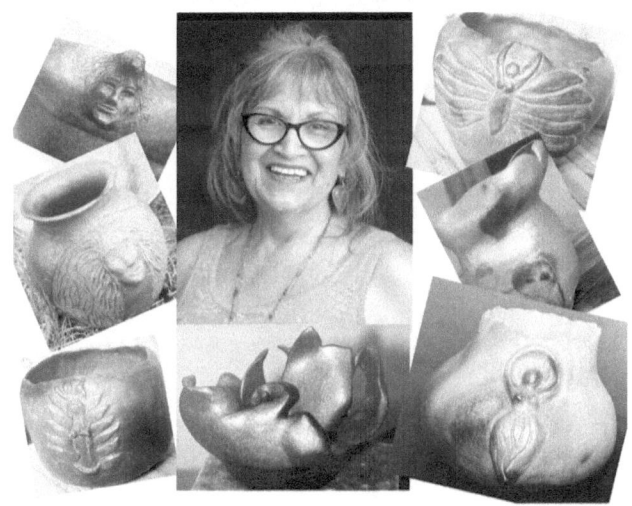

ABOUT THE AUTHOR

Selma is a Spiritual Connector who uses her unique Mother's Divine Essence to promote healing and well-being. Selma draws on her Indigenous lineage and sacred soul expansion that facilitates transformation and connection to provide spacious freedom from our mundane lifestyles.
As a Modern-Day Medicine Woman, She empowers women and helps them connect with their inner wisdom, cultivate self-love, and live in alignment with their soul's journey.

Selma offers services through her website, including one-on-one coaching, courses, and ancient vibrational energy medicine for healing. Selma's approach is holistically personal, and she works closely with each client to support them in their personalized way towards greater health, happiness, and spiritual fulfillment that impacts the world.

www.reikiyogamagic.com

CHAPTER 13
GODDESS ARIANRHOD

By: **DANIELLE SCHRECK**

Weaving New Earth Timeline with Goddess Arianrhod

Standing on the precipice of a great change can rattle even the most prepared. This world has been at war in places many unconsciously know about, which is what Humanity's current circumstances are: A Frequency War. These cosmic wars are coming online for many that have been "Awakening" for some time. Everything is Frequency, and we hold a Divine God Spark. Creator gifted us with a Frequency essence so unique that this war has been hidden for centuries but in some way told in various ways.

We are the anchor, light, and Frequency, a muse and guiding light. We are a community, and you find security within true connections rooted in love, and this love is showing up in ways to support this great shift.

The elements to create this requires you to stand with your brothers and sisters and not let fear or the illness of this world distract you. Your mind, body, and spirit are your trinity to uphold this foundation by channeling the Christ consciousness that streams through you. Guard it with your free will and intention. It is your sword of truth and love that will help the blind to suddenly see, releasing a blindfold that reveals the veil of illusions that create this mind control rooted in deception. It is this medicine we need during a time of great change, and the Goddesses are here to help activate and bring this essence into your whole being.

This World Seeks Sacred Leadership

Being honest and true to yourself is a priority as it sets the tone for whom you show up in this World. This World seeks leadership, and some still look outside themselves. Those aware of this intense moment in history are shown the depth of their being and the "remembrance" of the Divine Goddess, sacred sisterhood, sacred union, and sacred ways of "being." True leadership is the ability to take responsibility for oneself, so dare to lead your life in a frequency of great integrity, which stands as a bridge for others to do the same in their truth and integrity. A conscious sword of truth is fierce and creates inspiration as a match that lights one to shift and change so intensely that nothing outside can stop it. It is fully embodied with the power of its essence, and that force of nature cannot be stopped. This strength is accessible to all, and it is with great intention of sharing the wisdom of Goddess Arianrhod that I hope to ignite your "Inner Goddess" and empowerment of the supernatural ability to transform your destiny of past, present, future, and parallel lifetimes into the full embodiment of her essence.

Being a vessel of this level is one of the highest callings for your soul's evolution. We, the Goddess archetypes, are coming back online, and it's time to acknowledge and honor the wisdom and frequencies each keeper's key unlocks. Through compassion towards self, your surrender is a ripple effect that shifts each of us. Is this a moment in time that leaps many forward? That is not the concern but the hope in knowing that your great love, courage, and leadership create a change in yourself that extends to others, creating the possibilities of shifting fate to a reality of your chosen manifestation.

The perception of the challenges you experience are the challenges others experience, and as some wisdom keepers say: "There is no other-I am you, and you are me." This is a great saying to express the immense importance of frequency shift to this profound level of change. We, the divine frequency keepers, are online, re-coding a paradigm of the divine feminine power, strength, and beauty as many elements shine and shift this great time of reclaiming our sovereignty.

Calling Upon Goddess Arianrhod

I CALL UPON ARIANROD, the beautiful Celtic Goddess known as the Goddess of the Silver Wheel. It is time to anchor these codes to remember the Frequency you represent to help with this transition in Humanity. Your wheel of the year, birth, death, reincarnation, letting go of the past, initiation, feminine power, fertility, virginity, childbirth, and weaving of fate bring the re-coding of this aspect to help bring a level of empowered leadership to those seeking to gain support in shifting and creating these manifestations to a new earth.

You are a representation of portals to the land, sea, and sky, serving others as a Goddess of the otherworld. Bring forth your great wisdom as Humanity crosses the realms and lives to tell of these times of long-lived slavery, invertedness, and suffering. Give those who stand in their power the strength to hold this Frequency as this resurrection occurs in the death and rebirth of this world.

Your example of great strength in empowerment, inspiration, and transformation are gems we can download into our being while weaving a fate through these realms. Through the power of learning to stand up for ourselves, you have shown us how to weave our destiny as we all let go of the past. We reject others' attempts to control; we honor our fierce independence and autonomy through these codings. As the mother and life-giver, your devotion and patience nurture the choice to create our realm around cycles of time into our reality. A potent frequency that is with us along the journey.

STORIES OF THE GODDESS

Arianrhod is a Welsh Goddess who lived on an island off the west-coast of Wales. At the center of her castle was a turning glass tower containing the mystical Seat of Poetic Inspiration. Arianrhod uses her power of the Challenger, the power of the Initiator, with her deep wisdom to help bring great change. As one of the five Goddesses originating from the Isle of Avalon, Arionrhod brings magic into your life as you transform your destiny.

DANIELLE SCHRECK

ABOUT THE AUTHOR

Danielle is a passionate Empath who thrives on making

connections with people. She dedicates herself to hosting engaging interviews with holistic healers, where she delves into topics related to the Divine Feminine, Spiritual Awakening, and inspiration. Her mission is to inspire and empower individuals to believe in themselves, honoring their unique journeys and sharing their Conversations from the Heart. You can find these enriching conversations on her YouTube channel, "Conversations from the Heart."

With a specialty in Pendulum Healing, Danielle offers private sessions and Monthly Group Healing Events. She is a Graduate of Goddess Code Academy, where she attained certification as a Spinning Goddess™ Pendulum Healer. Danielle is also an accomplished Writer to several collaborative books: "Pillars of Light: Stories of Goddess Activations, Energy Healing and Soul Medicine Vol 2, and Infinite Cosmic Records: Sacred Doorways to Healing & Remembering." Her writing offers readers insight and wisdom into the mystical world of energy healing and spiritual awakening, produced by Radhaa Publishing House.

Find Danielle: @aphrodite.heart.vibes

CHAPTER 14
CATALYST TO THE DIVINE?

By: AMANDA WATERMAN

Fentanyl: A Spiritual Catalyst to the Divine?

I was receiving an energy healing from Sharon Doerr, and she asked me what I wanted to focus on. Usually, I would say whatever popped up that needed to be healed, but this time I told her I wanted to know why I was blocked from writing this chapter. We did an exercise where we invited God to come, and I could ask anything bothering me, hoping it would give me direction. I immediately asked God why I was being blocked from writing my chapter. He said it's because I would channel a specific message from God themselves. That took the pressure off of me. I channel all the time. Ancestors pop in and want to get messages for their loved ones that I am working with. My guides and angels pop in and give me messages. By far, this was a much bigger message. This a message for parents who have children addicted to drugs... specifically fentanyl.

As a mom with adult children addicted to fentanyl, I struggle with trying to take over and making them go to treatment or continuing to heal myself and trust that everything is perfect the way God intended it to be. So I step back and let them learn through the choices that they are making as hard as it is for me. My daughter has overdosed twice within one month from fentanyl and was revived by Narcan. My son also uses fentanyl but says his addiction doesn't affect anyone because he has never overdosed like many people. There is a balance between tough love and compassion.

Throughout motherhood, we embody different energies from different Goddesses along the way. Most of the time, we must be aware of what is happening. Lately, I've been working with the Goddess Shakti's energy. Shakti is the creator Goddess. She is the female aspect of cosmic energy. I automatically tap into this energy daily because I am Archangel Lady Faith, and my twin flame is Archangel Michael. In this chapter, you will read a conversation between Shakti and Lady Faith about the pressing issue of fentanyl.

Lady Faith: Shakti, is there a reason why there is such a need for young people to want to try fentanyl?

Shakti: Yes.

Lady Faith: What is that reason?

Shakti: It's to experience life in different realms, realms that they cannot obtain here.

Lady Faith: So they can "check out," so to speak, from this reality and visit other dimensions?

Shakti: Yes. This Earthly dimension is so dense, and they feel the most pain. Most of the younger generation are having such a hard time surviving here. Most are starseeds, angels, indigo children, etc., and being here alone, as they feel they are, is too much to bear. They have never felt like they belong anywhere. They have never felt the love that they think they deserve. It's different when you are one with us, source energy. You feel loved, whole, and complete. When they come to Earth, they feel alone, discarded by family, and deserted. They long for home.

Lady Faith: So the fentanyl epidemic is serving a purpose?

Shakti: Yes, it is serving them because they can tap into higher states of consciousness without someone judging them. They feel whole and complete... a state of bliss and oneness with source energy.

Lady Faith: But it ruins their physical life here on Earth, and they risk dying every time they decide to use it. People have lost their loved ones to overdoses.

Shakti: Yes, but I can assure you that they had no pain when they transitioned from the physical being back to the spiritual being. Every soul has to return to source energy where they are home once again. Every soul wants this, and when they return to that, they don't want to return to the Earth plane.

Lady Faith: Why would someone come to Earth and take a drug to leave Earth early?

Shakti: Only some people want to stay for long periods, and everyone has their blueprint with exit points for when they can choose to leave Earth and return to source energy. Every soul has to walk in their journey. No one else can walk it for them. There is so much more to it.

Lady Faith: Is it true that there is an entity that is attached to fentanyl?

Shakti: Good question! Why don't we ask Amanda to help answer that for us?

Lady Faith: Amanda, is there an entity attached to fentanyl?

Amanda: I get a yes!

Lady Faith: Okay, what is it?

Amanda: It is an offensive energy from other humans, but it's different for each individual. We would have to dig in more to find out. We need to heal the root trauma that created it to begin with. What came up when I asked the question, what is the entity attached to fentanyl? I got that dehydration plays a big role in addiction. Being dehydrated creates an imbalance in our bodies, causing us to be deficient in minerals.

AMANDA WATERMAN

ABOUT THE AUTHOR

Everyone comes across various types of challenges in their lives. Metaphysically speaking, these challenges come from other times in history, time points, and even other dimensions. ***Amanda Waterman*** has the gift to support you in healing and clearing these challenges so you can have the life you desire. As an Energy Healer, Angel Activator, Light

Worker, Life Coach, Mastermind Leader, Addiction Advocate, and business owner, Amanda has a long list of skills and gifts to elevate your life on every level. She is selfless beyond words and gives more than 100%, all while raising a family and caring for her senior clients. To work with Amanda, you can email her at clearcodingwithamanda@gmail.com

CHAPTER 15
LEMURIAN GODDESS MARIA MAKILING

By: **MAYA THE SHAMAN**

Earth Goddess - Maria Makiling

Maria Makiling is the Goddess of Lemuria. Lemuria is the lost continent of the Pacific. Maharlika (known as the Philippines) is a fragment of the lost continent of Mu or Lemuria. According to the legend, there was a deity or Goddess named Maria Makiling, a beautiful Earth brown skin nature Goddess with dark brown eyes and long black hair. She provided abundance and protection to the people. In the distant past, indigenous people called upon Maria Makiling to protect them from typhoons, earthquakes, and natural catastrophes. She lives in the mountains dedicated to her, called *"Maria Makiling,"* as the protector of the wilderness - the wild, and free animals.

But these days, people have forgotten about her offerings of abundance and protection, so they stopped affirming her presence in their lives because people have become used to feeling the daily grind of hardships after hundreds of non-stop years of colonization, where ongoing corrupt government politicians have been busy filling their sacks with stolen wealth from the people.

Though many have forgotten Maria Makiling as a protectress of people, she kept the poachers out of her mountain to safeguard her animal kingdom. She has been seen sitting nearby spring waters and peacefully spending time with nature's animals or moving across the tall grassy reeds as if flying.

When someone comes across with bad intentions to hurt or kill her animals, she pretends to be an animal to distract, confuse, and eliminate the shooter by losing his way in the forest. On the other hand, Maria Makiling offers protection and guidance to others who come across with good intentions and respect towards nature. Once, a lost traveler came across Maria Makiling; she helped guide him to find his way back home and gifted him with her *"Ginger roots."* He happily walked home with gratitude, thinking of the kind lady but found his travel back home slow. Carrying the ginger roots got heavier and heavier. He felt the weight of every step, so he started to unload the ginger roots and threw them one by one on the path, leaving just enough for his family to use for a few meals. When he got home, to his surprise, he found his ginger roots had turned into gold, and by that time, a great realization had come upon him. *"He met an enchanted deity, a Goddess —A giver of abundance."* With humility, he knew he was abundantly blessed by the Goddess Maria Makiling's presence but did not have the resilience to keep moving forward.

Lesson of Resilience

The lesson I learned from this story is, *"No matter how much heavy-weight one carries on their shoulders for having difficulty in one's life path, the great provider of blessings watches over, testing our resilience and waiting for that perfect moment to provide the golden opportunity of protection and abundance."* So no matter how difficult one may have been going through in one's life struggles, there will be a time of blessings, protection, and abundance from this Goddess of Nature, Maria Makiling — the Lemurian Earth Mother Gaia herself.

The Mountain of Maria Makiling

I was born in the same province where Maria Makiling resides, Los Banos Laguna (Philippines), where the people once revered the ancestral deity. Once upon a time people knew they could ask for favors from their deities, keeping them in alignment with highest best through high yield of crops, good rains to nourish the Earth, fortune, or ask for protection. Godly in nature, the people experienced the higher frequency of their lineage working with the spirit realm. Ancestors reminded people of stories told by word of mouth passed down from one generation to the next in remembrance of the enchanted realms and sacredness of the land they call *"Inang Bayan* meaning *Motherland."* The original indigenous people of this land, the sacred land keepers, and our ancestors carried the template with qualities of abundance and sacredness — it was the Lemurian way. But slowly, the culture eroded, forgetting who they were.

The Exploitation of the Land and People of Mu

Since the conquering of Spain several hundred years ago with sword and cross, Catholicism was imposed. The sacred culture slowly went downhill despite the struggle to keep their desired ideals. The deity-ancestral worship was chopped to the core, diminished, and its power was mostly forgotten. After WW2, Spain, Japan, and the USA got a hold of Maharlika and lost it too because people revolted and were tired of being slaved repeatedly in their homeland! The true reality of the Divine wealth of the land and its people slipped through the cracks of poverty and into the hands of corrupt political leaders and exploiters of natural resources.

Lemuria and its noble Maharlikan race are coming back online to claim sovereign rights over their ownership of their identity, and riches - its authentic natural wealth is its true identity. Maharlika was once the richest country on Earth, rich in culture, talented and service-minded people, plenty of gold, abundant natural resources, and ruled by Kings and Queens (only a few people on Earth knew this). Because of the great hospitality and service-mindedness of the people, they were easily taken advantage of and *"Stolen from in broad daylight,"* says Queen Helen Abdurajak of the Maharlika

Empire. Those who knew who they were now claim back their rightful sovereign heritage.

As our World transitions from Dark Matrix to Light and Truth, there will be an awakening by the masses, and for Lemuria, the Lemurians are awakening like no other!

What is the *"Divine Wealth"* that awaits towards the Golden Age of Mu? Before this great shift could occur, the land and governing people of Maharlika needed to come clean politically and economically so that the Divine Wealth could be distributed with Peace to the people. Yet, hoping for a greater change, the past country's corrupt leaders slowly dismantled whatever authentic power was left to the people. Every corrupt Filipino President who stepped into office sold some islands to China for years. Claiming back the islands from the mess created by these corrupt leaders is looking more and more like a War zone.

World Leaders Fighting for Control Over Resources in the Pacific

The year 2023 has looked more like a *'nuclear nightmare'* being waved in the air as threats caused by both China and the USA. Like spoiled little boys playing with detrimental toys causing low frequency and fear in our planet. First, China has been using the Philippines as a strategic location for multiple uses to claim natural resources and expand its territory with nearby Taiwan. In addition to its aggressive bullish nature, it also interferes with neighboring countries; Vietnam, Japan, and Indonesia. Second, the USA is in the same league, with similar agendas. It wants to use the Philippine islands for its strategic war base and look for resources (natural or otherwise) in competition with China's claim over Taiwan - the top producer of microchips used in our phones & etc. These claimants want to have resources they cannot peacefully talk about. Instead, they use the power of manipulation, control, and war threats to disturb World peace.

Concerned Americans with War Drama in the Pacific

The imbalance between the nurturing divine feminine and protective divine masculine is again being sabotaged by corroding Patriarchal ways. The US military asking for billions of dollars from the US government to support them with the strongest war weapons, announcing a premeditated War projected in 2025-2026 is simply over the top. Who do you think would pay the billions of dollars for this USA War in the Pacific? Of course, the People of America! Is this why part of the solution by the US government to gain monetary funds was to control banks and people's money and then replace it with digital currency to keep track of people's power spending and control people? Wouldn't citizens have known about this if it's not being leaked out? According to sources I discovered, the same government advisors who worked closely with the government themselves are going online to warn people. If a premeditated plan rolled out, it would look like instant communism in America - China and USA would look exactly alike! Go figure. As a citizen of the

World, everyone should know. I am not a bringer of negative news. I want to be aware.

Just imagine if you're bringing the War from the West to the East, saying: *"to maintain the freedom of navigation in the Pacific!"* Is this the highest and best good for everyone or just for a few? The US says they have no plans for a long-term stay in the Philippines, yet, the Filipino people I've known do not believe it, for no country would invest millions to billions of dollars and pull out the next day!

The USA proposed nine military infrastructure bases in the Philippines with a budget of 82 million dollars and asked for more, by the billions, to go to War. With the 17 thousand US soldiers already deployed in the Philippines, navy war fleets, warships, artilleries, bombers, jets, war trucks, proposed nuclear bombs, and all types of war gadgets with the hopes of conducting a winning War against China, will the US really help the Philippines from China's claim to the West Philippine Sea? How long will they stay in the Philippines?

War hunger is a dirty business. It tells humanity that destructive greed and powers are in the wrong hands. Actions made by ourselves or others can affect our immediate relationships and others. While our leaders' actions affect massively the greater part of humanity — our World. The Patriarch is war-mongering and rotten leaders pushing us toward disaster!

I was so upset. I sat in my meditation, and after deep contemplation, I realized this timeline of War was over! The great Creator of this grand Universe has another plan. I asked my higher self, is there something I can do?

The Art of Spiritual Warfare & People's Power

To look deeper into spirituality, these very dark actions created in our World are no longer allowed by the great Universe. A time of change is upon us.

While writing this, I am reminded that everything must pass. Our Earth people have endured so much pain and suffering throughout the ages. In our lifetime, we have seen a lot! Personally and collectively, we have witnessed harsh realities in our timeline. Lies and blankets of darkness made many people blind, while ears plugged up with old beliefs could not hear the truth. Yet, in each passing moment, I have learned "thoughts and actions" are needed to infuse what we desire to create in our World. Have you ever asked yourselves what we want to see to create a brighter future for us and humanity?

How do we create a Massive Shift of Consciousness During this Spiritual Warfare?

As we decide to shift our consciousness to return to our most natural way of being, we will create a World that has no desire for War but desires only to create Peace, happiness, and prosperity for all. A new way of being fully embodied in our hearts, mind, and souls, bringing us closer to our *"Divine Spiritual Wealth"* supported by the great Universe.

A time when deep contemplation, meditation, stretching the body, breath work, affirmations, and healing our wounds can find our way back to our *'Internal Peace,'* creating high frequency and answers that can be found in silence (without 3D denial). Light-workers, Starseeds, Peacekeepers — together, we can ask assistance from our guides, Enchanted Beings, Ascended Masters, Gods, and Goddesses of this Universe and Multiverse as our allies - *"One planet, One human family."* Those not aligned with this highest truth will find themselves elsewhere.

The power of intention creates magic. When done with great numbers of people on Earth, it can be like white laser beams of light stronger than any nuclear explosion and can create positive waves of protection and unstoppable healing in our World. As the veil is thinning. if done sincerely daily, it can dissolve dark War energies. Counteract dark magic with Infinite light force. It's the *"Power of white magic against black magic."*

The Cosmic Truth

There is only one highest truth. The ultimate God/Goddess is one and the same, *"Like the palm and back of the hand, God/Goddess are inseparable,"*- says an ascended Master Anandamurtiji.

The Gods and Goddesses came to Earth to share, teach, and remind humanity to bring back the balance between the Divine Feminine and Divine masculine. We are being asked to open our hearts and minds and work together to collectively clean dark energies and shadowy spaces on Earth, internally and externally. This is what spiritual warfare meant to me at this timeline in our Earth's history. We are **Bridging** the gap to **Remembering** *"Herstory"* to balance the deficiencies in *"History."*

At the level of advanced AI technology, humans cannot fully comprehend the horrific destructive advancement of Wars and what they can do, nor the positive transcending advanced bright future awaiting us if given a chance! To continue having War on planet Earth is insanity and the highest form of self-sabotage, resulting in self-annihilation for those who continue this destructive path. When War is no longer an option, what would it look like a hundred years from now?

Lemuria is Rising

There's a saying from our elders in Lemuria *"We are the first and will be the last."* According to the Lemurians, being the first continent on planet Earth, the sacred guardians of Lemuria have been installed in this land to live long lives to witness the events. They knew the Cosmic story, so they went underground and created the Crystal Lemurian Kingdom beneath the Pacific Ocean. Their powers were not reduced to 3D-like humans who live on Earth's surface. The Dark forces have experimented with surface humans through DNA manipulations and multiple traumatic circumstances. Forgetting who they were - Divine! Now it is time for us to remember, come back to zero point.

From The Age of Darkness to The Age of Light & Truth

THE END IS the beginning of a new cycle. From *Kali Yuga* (Dark Ages) to *Satya Yuga* (Age of Light & Truth), we are in our transition period called *Yugasandhi,* where internal and external old systems must be cleansed - from corrupt politics, financial manipulation, lies, etc. - a total renewal, a systematic spiritual launching of new governance for the people and by the people.

Theory Made Practical

The closest theory I encountered describes a beautiful vision close to my Heart, practical and clearly laid out by a spiritual ascended Master, Shrii Shrii Anandamurtiji, before he left his Earthly body. It is called *Progressive Utilization Theory* (PROUT). A futuristic spiritual solution and a well-balanced system to reorganize our society.

This theory can be a practical experience in reality as one of its foundations is based on the equal participation of both women and men in building a balanced socio-economic reality. The ascended Master inspires Women to know their role and importance in society, uplift their positioning and dignity in the societal sphere of influence, and step forward in a grounded benevolent leading force.

Women will rise by using the faculties of their hearts, minds, and spirit to transcend limitations in establishing a divine feminine leadership. There will be progress as women and men work on clearing their weaknesses while gaining internal strength. In an orderly society, the confidence of divine feminine and divine masculine leadership are assets. Any misunderstandings can be resolved, restored, and respected through a dialogue and higher spiritual frequency of self-reflections to create harmony and Peace on Earth.

Reflections

"The reflection of our inner World is the expression of our external World. It's an inward movement we are being asked to make now. Our prayer is our internal conversation with the Supreme God/Goddess to hold the highest sacred space for humanity on planet Earth. Our job is to invite the Supreme God/Goddess to our home, our sacred hearts, be ready to receive the new Earth free from chaos. I call upon the Lemurian Goddess Maria Makiling for her protection of our Earth's people, animals, and nature. Shower your abundant Peace and rich natural resources for the highest good and best outcome for all - as we recognize full appreciation for your divine gifts. It is my greatest intention that the light and unconditional love of the Prime Source Creator with allied Gods and Goddesses carry us across from the most intense timeline of darkness toward the other side of this realm as we enter the pure light of the Lemurian Golden Age for all of humanity to enjoy. So be it."

Aho!
Salamat po.
~Maya The Shaman

MAYA THE SHAMAN

ABOUT THE AUTHOR

Maya Verzonilla, aka *Maya The Shaman*, is a visionary Lemurian Shaman, energy healer, and author known for her innovative, original healing modalities - Lemurian Code Healing (LCH) & Infinite Cosmic Records (ICR). Her work blends the wisdom of the East with the needs of the West, bridging ancient practices with modern Healing.

Maya The Shaman is the author of the book, **"Infinite Cosmic Records: Sacred Doorways to Healing & Remembering"** and co-authored several best-selling books: Energy Healing & Soul Medicine, Awakening Starseeds Vol. 1,2,3, Pillars of Light and Stories of the Goddess. Maya founded the Lemurian Code Academy, teaching and guiding students her Healing modalities, ICR & LCH. She was featured in the documentary film "The Cure," alongside Deepak Chopra and Marianne Williamson, produced by Sharon Stone and directed by French Director Emmanuel Itier. Another documentary film she's seen, "Guns, Bombs, and War: A Love Story," where Maya stands as a powerful voice for peace.

Maya The Shaman's work has also been featured in LA Formidable Magazine, where she was interviewed and recognized as a formidable woman. She is a teacher, mentor, and beacon of hope for all seeking to heal and remember their true essence in her widely known icon **HBR "Heart-Bridging-Remembering"** as part of her original healing modalities, Infinite Cosmic Records & Lemurian Code Healing.

Find Maya The Shaman at www.MayaTheShaman.com or email her at LemurianCodeHealing@gmail.com.

ABOUT RADHAA PUBLISHING HOUSE

BECOME AN AUTHOR
BECOME A CONTRIBUTING WRITER

Radhaa Publishing House is a holistic publishing company that focuses on helping heart-centered, mind-expanding, truth-telling authors get their work out into the world. Our focus is on collaborative book series and memoirs. We thrive on supporting our authors and contributing writers throughout this journey, empowering them to step into their divine and an authentic voice while sharing their truth with the world. We especially celebrate cultural diversity worldwide, and we believe in weaving international voices to come together.

HOW ARE WE DIFFERENT?

ABOUT RADHAA PUBLISHING HOUSE

Many collaborative publishing companies bundle the authors together so that they don't receive individual credit and acknowledgment. We make sure each Author is seen and heard and can be found easily. This has led to authors telling us that they have received more traffic and business and clients on their websites. In a sense, each of the Book we create is also like a Directory highlighting contributing writers unique offerings. This has been a win-win for the contributing writers and authors.

Here is what our authors have said about working with us:

"I felt totally supported. The best bit was feeling like being part of a loving family who wants you to be your best, do your best, and is there for you every step of the way. It also boosted my confidence as a writer. The collaborative nature of the project also made it way more fun than doing things alone".
    *- **Arrameia, Prague***

*"Visibility was a big piece of me coming out of the spiritual closet, and I felt that Radhaa Publishing House has a high energy and integrity level. Both of which are important for light workers and Starseeds. The curators and authors are light workers. Radhaa Publishing House created this wonderful opportunity for many others to be a part of. I felt that they put their whole heart into making this happen even before, during, and after the book is published. It was a project that was totally supportive that made me feel safe to share myself and my story." - **Lalitah, Turkey***

ABOUT RADHAA PUBLISHING HOUSE

"It was wonderful to work with Radhaa Publishing House. I saw the effort and perseverance the whole team has and the support system they have for all the authors. I have matured as an author from this experience. I was so inspired after writing my chapter in this book, Awakening Starseeds, that I wrote an entire book called The Great Awakening because I was deeply moved writing."

   - Leshara, Philippines

"My story was edited by Radhaa Publishing House, and let me tell you, it put me in tears! They made it better than the way I originally wrote and submitted it while keeping my story and voice true to its events. I read it, and tears just flowed because it was so good!"- **Cristal, Florida**

"I have published many books on Consciousness, empowerment subjects, and relationships, but I had never revealed raw, real stories of my life as with Awakening Starseeds. I wanted to join other authors writing personal stories, and Radhaa Publishing House made it simple and empowering to share from my heart in a real, raw way. This team of conscious, awesome Starseeds encourages a revolution to Awaken other Starseeds worldwide!" - **Stasia, Utah**

This is an opportunity to STEP OUT, SPEAK OUR TRUTHS. This is our time, an obligation to share and support others that live in fear and question their soul paths, their soul journey. - **Breda, Canada**

ABOUT RADHAA PUBLISHING HOUSE

At **Radhaa Publishing House,** we are highly involved in the entire process and work personally with the authors to navigate authorship challenges.

Our authors are heart-centered, soul-driven, and ready to manifest their legacy. We acknowledge the courage and strength it takes to step out into the public eye, and our team is here to support you all the way.

Creating a book is a tedious process and requires persistence, patience, and perspective. There are many moving parts of the book that need attention, and our team knows how to work hard to ensure we can come through with flying colors for the final date of our release.

Step into your voice and be heard now! When you become a contributing writer or an author of Radhaa Publishing House, you empower yourself in a way you may have never experienced before. That's what our authors tell us. Claim your author power now!

"Be that change you wanted to be in our world!"

If you have a compelling story to share with the world, dream of being a published author, and wish to be a part of the Radhaa Publishing family, reach out to us.

"No other publishing company offers you in-house support the way that Radhaa Publishing House does. Your legacy awaits!"

ABOUT RADHAA PUBLISHING HOUSE

To find out more information about how to Join us, Become an Author or See our Upcoming Books, please visit our Website at:
www.RadhaaPublishingHouse.com
Email: RadhaaPublishing@gmail.com

&

To Order a Signed Copies of our Books, visit our Online Store: https://radhaanilia.net/shop/
Email us: RadhaaPublishing@gmail.com

Thank you!

ABOUT RADHAA PUBLISHING HOUSE

You Make a Difference When You Support Our Holistic Books!

Published Books:
    Awakening Starseeds:
    Shattering Illusions, Vol.1

Awakening Starseeds:
    Stories Beyond The Stargate, Vol. 2

Awakening Starseeds:
    Dreaming into the Future, Vol. 3

Pillars of Light:
    Stories of Goddess Activations™

Energy Healing & Soul Medicine

Quan Yin Goddess Activations™
    Healing Workbook

Infinite Cosmic Records:
    Sacred Doorways to Healing
    & Remembering

Stories of the Goddess:
    Divine Feminine Frequency Keepers

Dolphin Oddssey

Forthcoming Books:

Poems From the Heart

Mahárliká: In Search of Identity

Embracing Aloha

Time is Promised to No One

Honor Time

Conductor of Time

Memoirs of a Galactic Goddess - 2nd edition

Descendants of Lemuria: Memoir

ABOUT RADHAA PUBLISHING HOUSE

WHERE YOU CAN FIND RADHAA PUBLISHING HOUSE BOOKS:

Amazon.com
Barnes and Noble
Target
Walmart
Powell Books
Radhaa Publishing House
&
Get your Signed Copy at Radhaa Publishing House

Email: RadhaaPublishing@gmail.com
Thank you for your support!

ABOUT RADHAA PUBLISHING HOUSE

TO OUR READERS:

Dear Readers,

I are am deeply humbled and grateful for your decision to invest your precious time in reading this book. Your presence here is not taken for granted, but rather cherished and celebrated. You are more than a mere reader; you are an esteemed companion on this extraordinary journey of self-discovery and empowerment as we delve into the captivating STORIES OF THE GODDESS.

In this pivotal moment of humanity's awakening, your soul consciously seeks to embrace the power of your femininity. This choice reflects your inherent wisdom and the invaluable contributions you make to the rejuvenation and transformation of our Earth. Your purpose, dear reader, extends far beyond your current understanding, intricately interwoven into the very fabric of human evolution and ascension.

As our world undergoes profound shifts and a new Earth takes shape, your compassionate leadership and enlightened thinking play a vital role in birthing a future where harmony, prosperity, and conscious awareness thrive. The significance of this transformative era cannot be overstated—it serves as a testament to the divine importance of your soul and a gentle reminder of the profound impact you have on the world around you.

With the utmost sincerity, I extend to you an invitation—a call to action—to unlock the ancient feminine wisdom nestled within the pages of the STORIES OF THE GODDESS. Now is the time to remember, to reconnect with your true essence, and reclaim your rightful place in the grand tapestry of life. Embrace your inherent divinity and remain steadfast in the certainty of your role in shaping the future of our world.

Together, with open hearts and united spirits, let us rise above and beyond, for within our collective power lies the boundless potential to create a future that surpasses our wildest dreams. I humbly ask you to share your experiences, insights, and reflections by leaving positive reviews that not only amplify the profound significance of this book but also inspire others to embark on their own transformative journeys.

Once again, I express my deepest gratitude for joining us on this path of self-discovery and empowerment. Together, let us illuminate the world with the radiance of our authentic selves. Together we RISE!

With Love, *Radhaa*

If you like our book

STORIES OF THE GODDESS

Please support us by leaving a review.

REVIEW us ONLINE at: Amazon.com.

ABOUT RADHAA PUBLISHING HOUSE

We cannot do this without your support! Share our journey with others!

With Love & Gratitude,
Thank you!

ABOUT RADHAA PUBLISHING HOUSE

REVIEW this Book ONLINE at: Amazon.com.

STORIES OF THE GODDESS

We can't do it without your loving support!

Many Blessings and Thank You!
Radhaa Publishing House

www.ingramcontent.com/pod-product-compliance
Lightning Source LLC
Chambersburg PA
CBHW030150100526
44592CB00009B/213